SAVAIS-TU ?
Les Marmottes

SAVAIS-TU ?
Les Marmottes

Alain M. Bergeron
Michel Quintin
Sampar

Illustrations de Sampar

ÉDITIONS
MICHEL
QUINTIN

Catalogage avant publication de Bibliothèque et Archives nationales du Québec et Bibliothèque et Archives Canada

Bergeron, Alain M.

Les marmottes

(Savais-tu?)
Éd. originale: 2010.
Pour enfants de 7 ans et plus.
ISBN 978-2-89435-555-8

1. Marmottes - Ouvrages pour la jeunesse. 2. Marmottes - Ouvrages illustrés - Ouvrages pour la jeunesse. I. Quintin, Michel. II. Sampar. III. Titre. IV. Collection: Bergeron, Alain M.. Savais-tu?.

QL737.R68B46 2012   j599.36'6   C2011-942385-5

Le Conseil des Arts du Canada
The Canada Council for the Arts

SODEC Québec

Patrimoine canadien
Canadian Heritage

La publication de cet ouvrage a été réalisée grâce au soutien financier du Conseil des Arts du Canada et de la SODEC. De plus, les Éditions Michel Quintin reconnaissent l'aide financière du gouvernement du Canada par l'entremise du Fonds du livre du Canada pour leurs activités d'édition.

Gouvernement du Québec – Programme de crédit d'impôt pour l'édition de livres – Gestion SODEC

Tous droits de traduction et d'adaptation réservés pour tous les pays. Toute reproduction d'un extrait quelconque de ce livre, par procédé mécanique ou électronique, y compris la microreproduction, est strictement interdite sans l'autorisation écrite de l'éditeur.

ISBN 978-2-89435-555-8

Dépôt légal – Bibliothèque et Archives nationales du Québec, 2012
Dépôt légal – Bibliothèque et Archives Canada, 2012

© Copyright 2012

Éditions Michel Quintin
C. P. 340, Waterloo (Québec)
Canada J0E 2N0
Tél.:   450 539-3774
Téléc.: 450 539-4905
editionsmichelquintin.ca

12-WKT-1

Imprimé en Chine

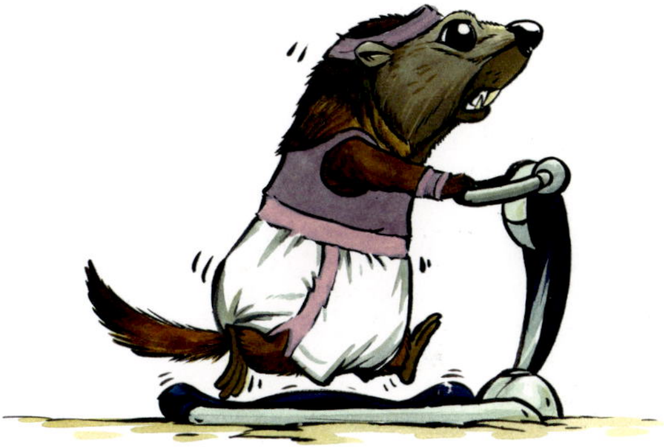

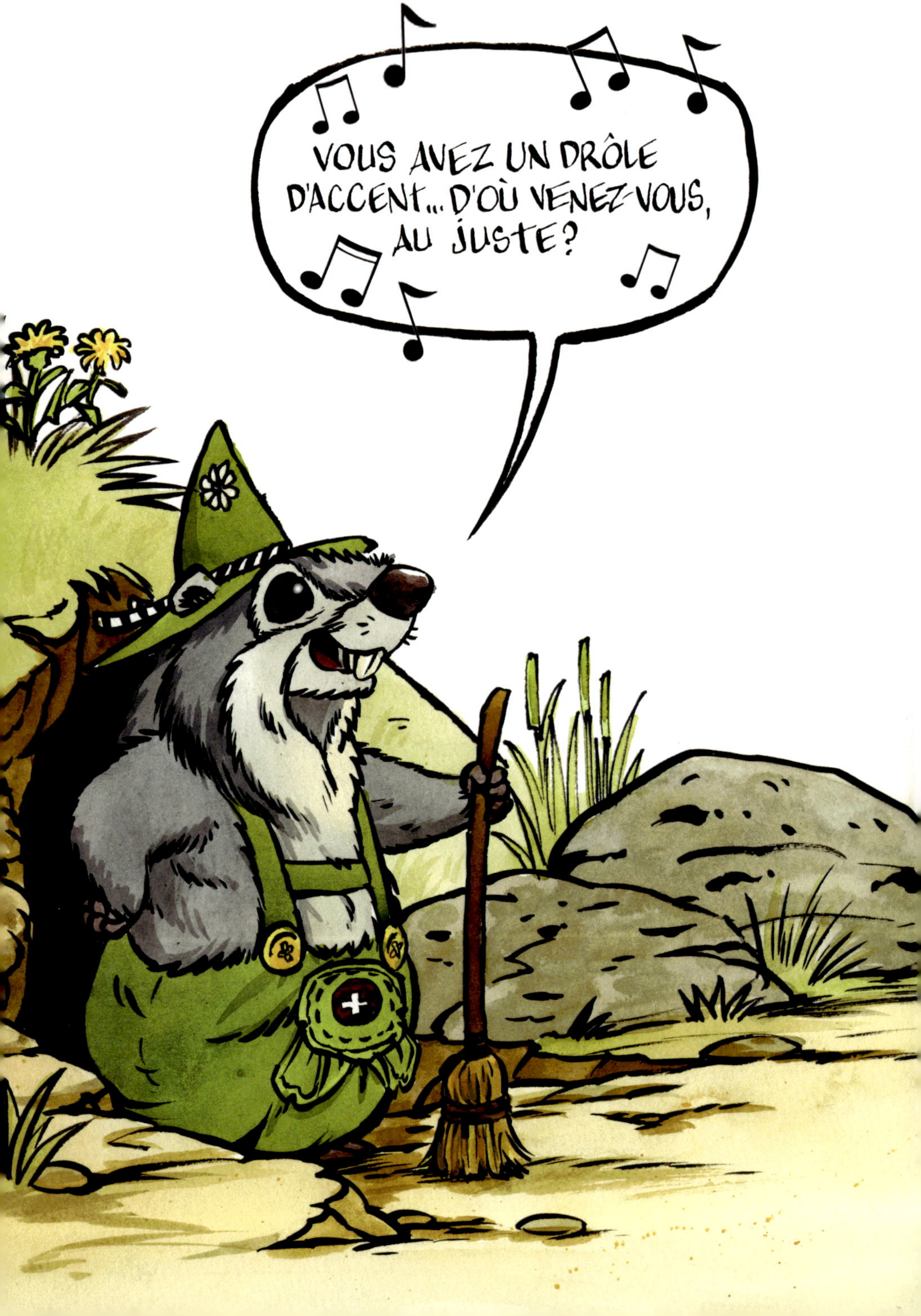
VOUS AVEZ UN DRÔLE D'ACCENT... D'OÙ VENEZ-VOUS, AU JUSTE?

« D'un p'tit trou, au Québec. »

Savais-tu qu'il existe 14 espèces de marmottes et qu'elles vivent toutes dans les régions froides de l'hémisphère Nord ? Ces espèces se ressemblent toutes beaucoup.

Savais-tu que ces gros rongeurs ont quatre puissantes incisives taillées en biseau ? Ces dents très tranchantes poussent et s'usent tout au long de leur vie.

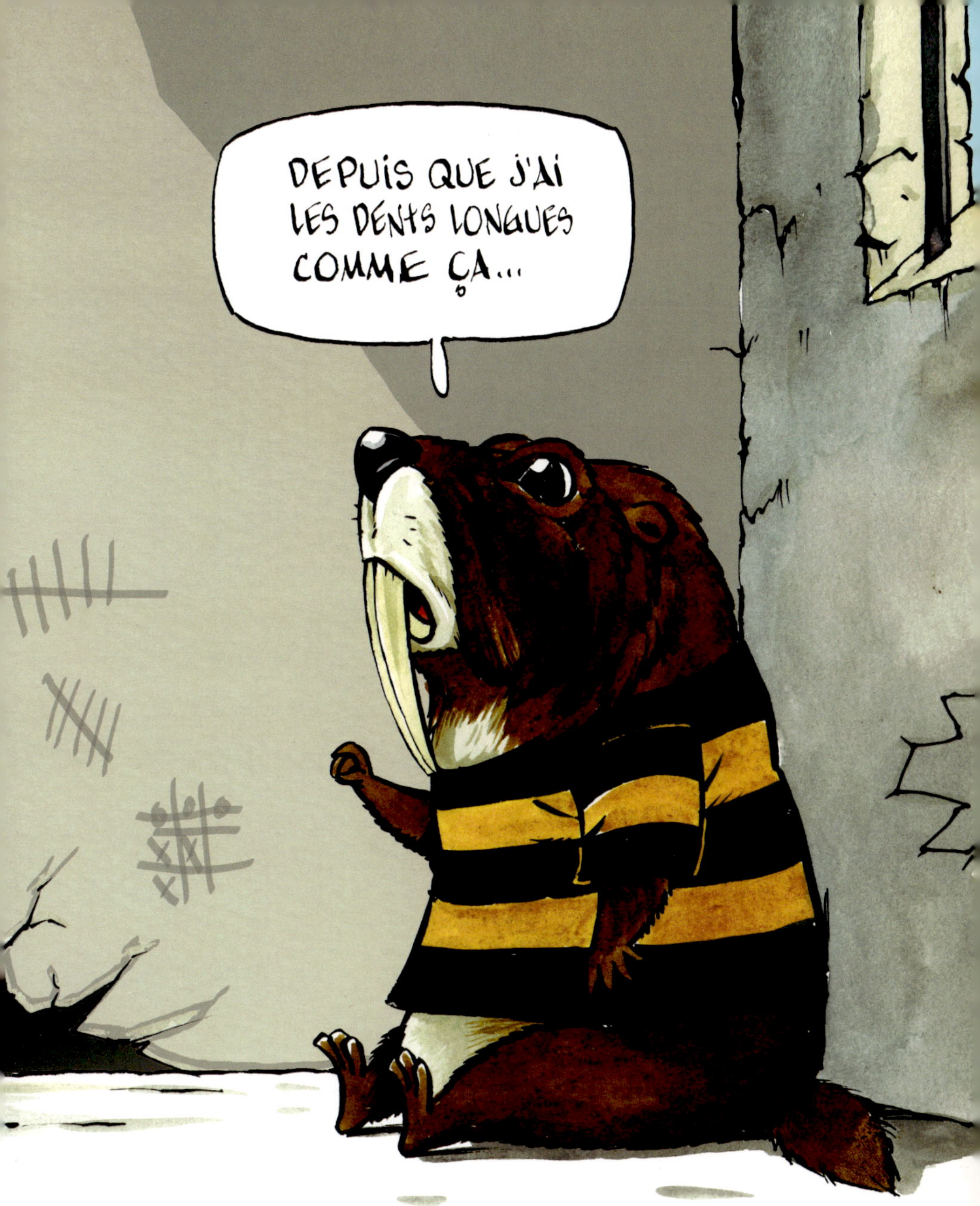
DEPUIS QUE J'AI LES DENTS LONGUES COMME ÇA...

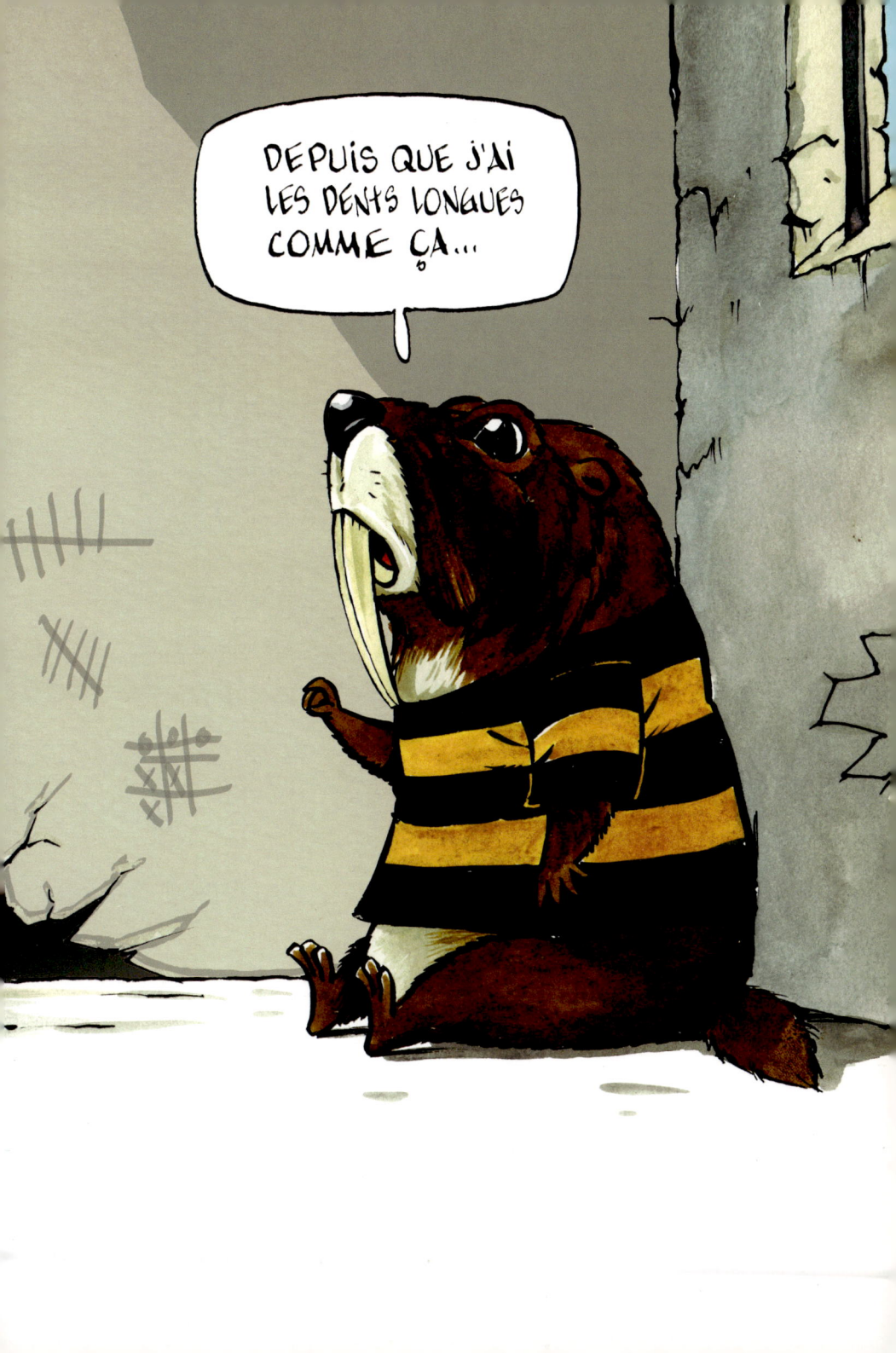

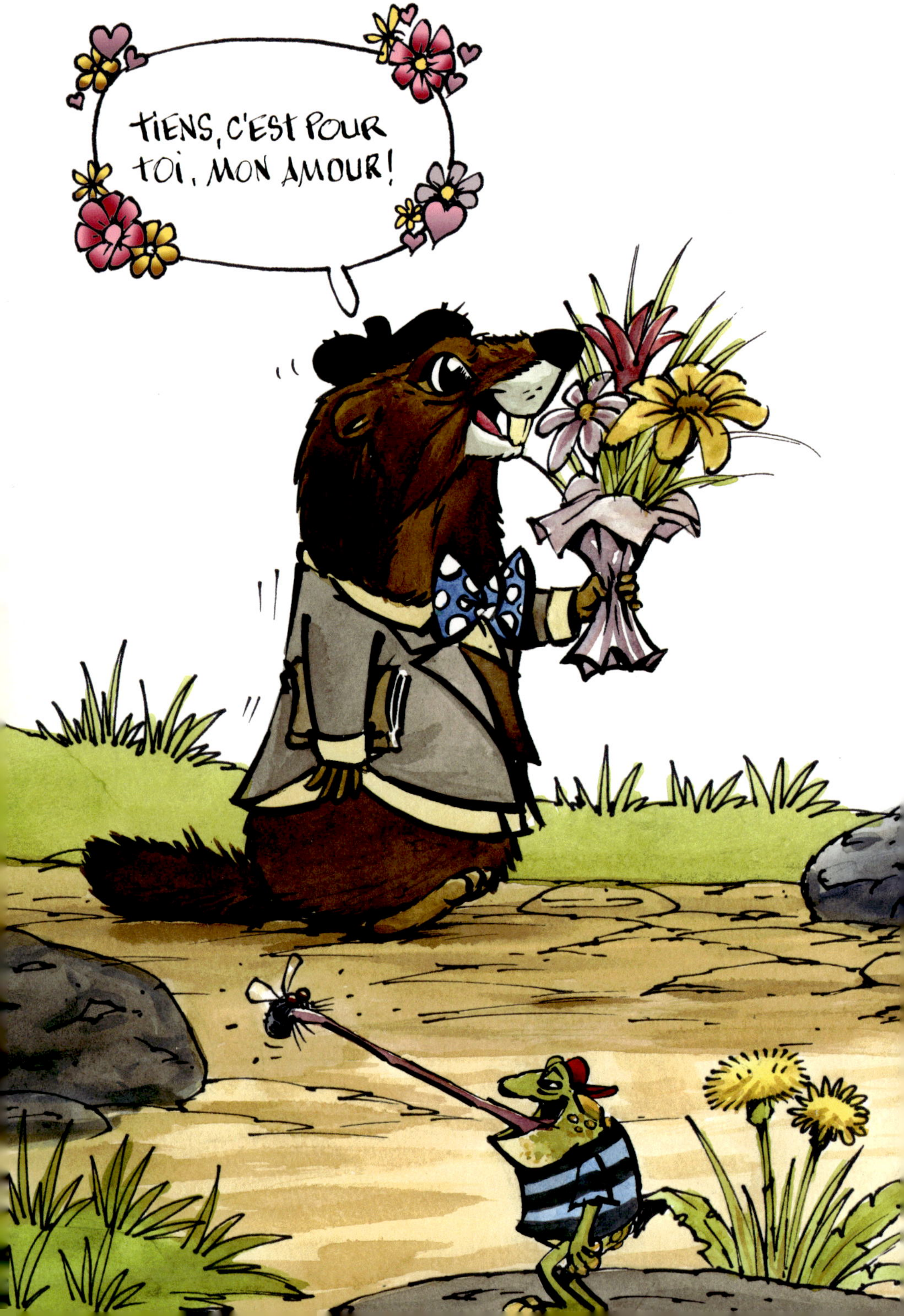
TIENS, C'EST POUR TOI, MON AMOUR!

Savais-tu que la marmotte se nourrit de fleurs, d'herbes et de fruits ? Cet herbivore consomme aussi à l'occasion des vers, des insectes et des œufs.

Savais-tu que la marmotte ingurgite environ 500 grammes de nourriture quotidiennement? Chez l'homme, ce serait l'équivalent de 6 kilos d'aliments par jour.

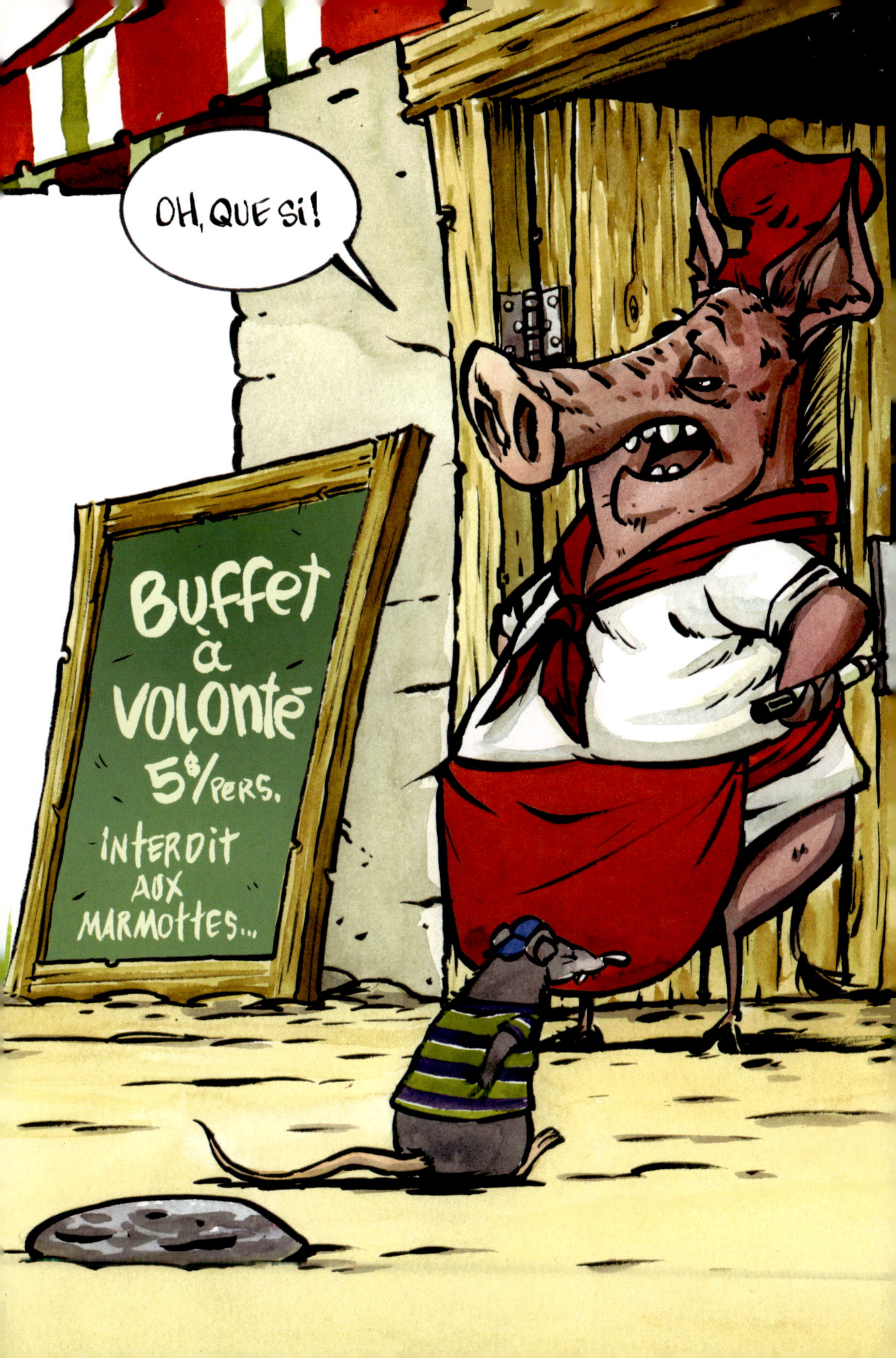
OH, QUE SI!
Buffet à volonté
5$/pers.
interdit aux marmottes...

POUAH! ON DEVINE CE QUE TU AS MANGÉ POUR DÎNER...
TU VEUX DE LA GOMME?

Savais-tu que la marmotte est cæcotrophe ? Cela signifie qu'elle mange certaines de ses crottes et digère ainsi ses aliments une seconde fois.

Savais-tu que c'est un mammifère strictement diurne, qui adore passer de longs moments à se chauffer au soleil ?

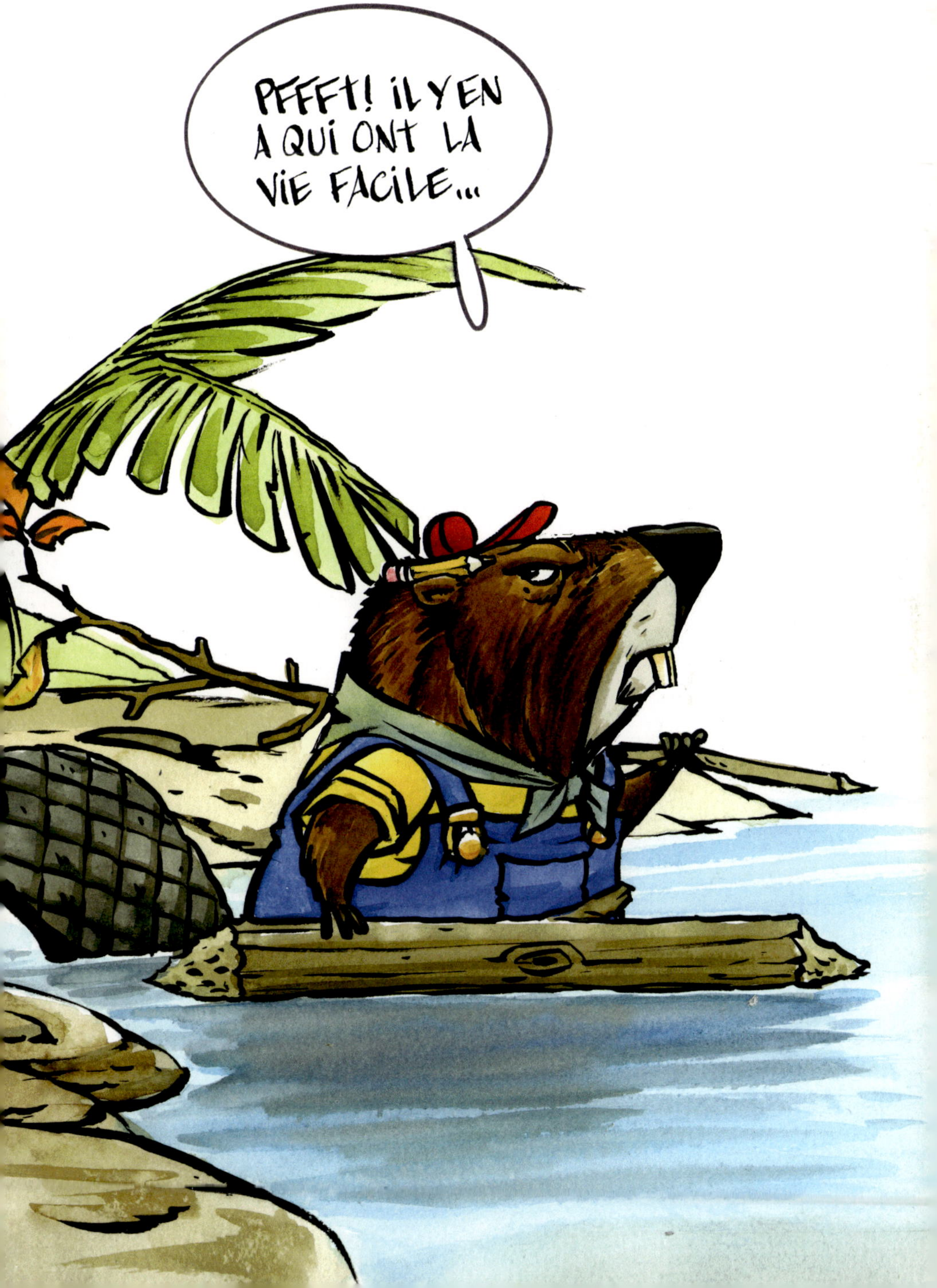
PFFFT! IL Y EN A QUI ONT LA VIE FACILE...

JE NE ME SENS PAS BIEN, TOUT À COUP. TON REPAS DÉGAGE UNE FORTE ODEUR...
LE PETIT COIN, C'EST PAR LÀ ?

Savais-tu que cet animal fouisseur habite dans un terrier ? Son abri, composé habituellement de deux pièces dont une chambre principale et une autre lui servant de toilette, comprend plusieurs issues.

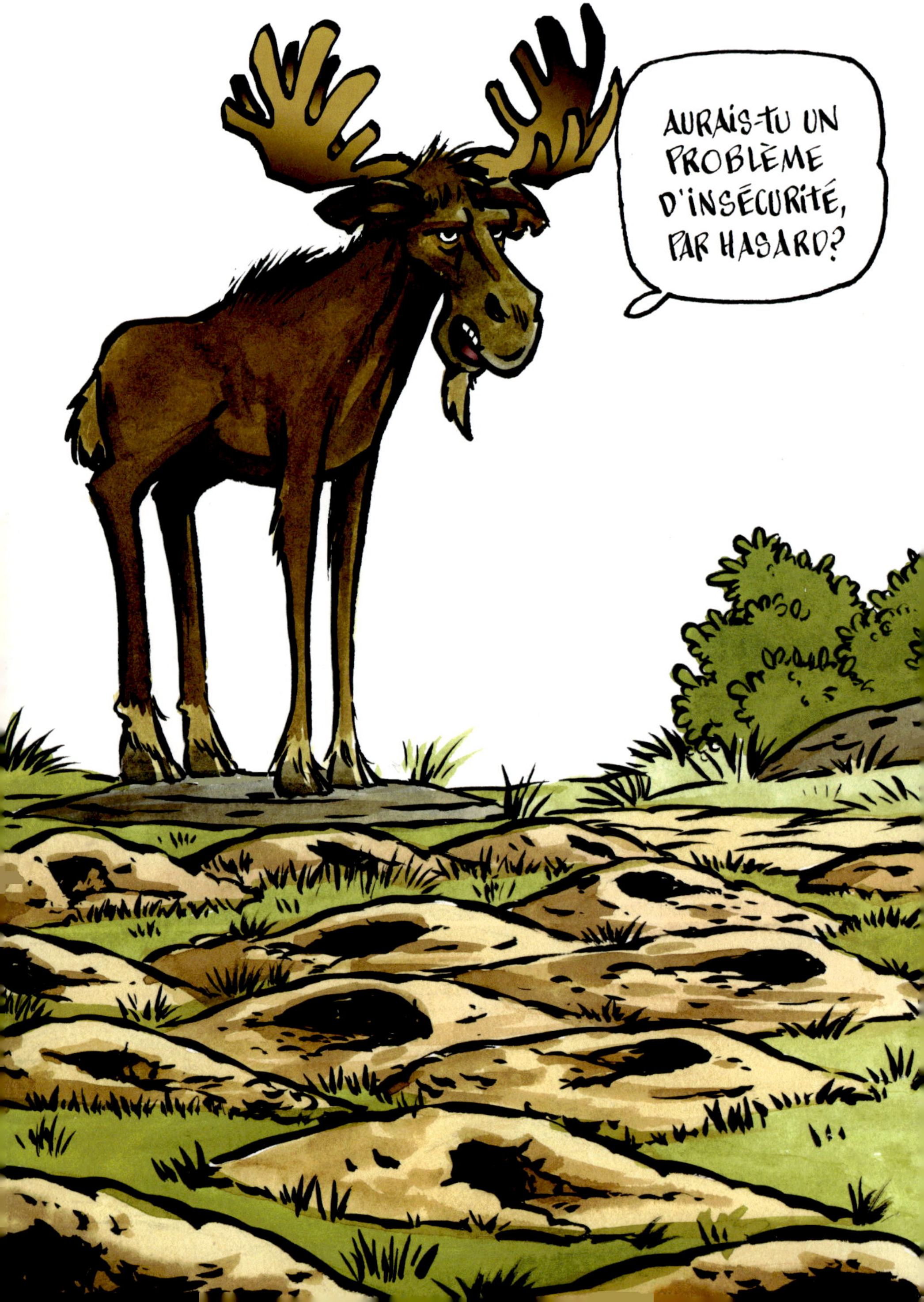
AURAIS-TU UN PROBLÈME D'INSÉCURITÉ, PAR HASARD?

Savais-tu que la marmotte creuse des trous peu profonds un peu partout sur son territoire ? Ils lui serviront de cachettes en cas d'urgence.

> À CHAQUE FOIS QUE JE METS LE MUSEAU DEHORS, J'AI L'IMPRESSION QU'ON VEUT ME BOUFFER...
>
> VOUS COMPRENEZ CE QUE JE VEUX DIRE, DOCTEUR?

Savais-tu que les marmottes, qu'elles vivent en montagne ou dans les plaines, choisissent toujours un endroit dégagé pour élire domicile? Constamment sur le qui-vive, elles se dressent sur leurs pattes arrière pour mieux surveiller les alentours.

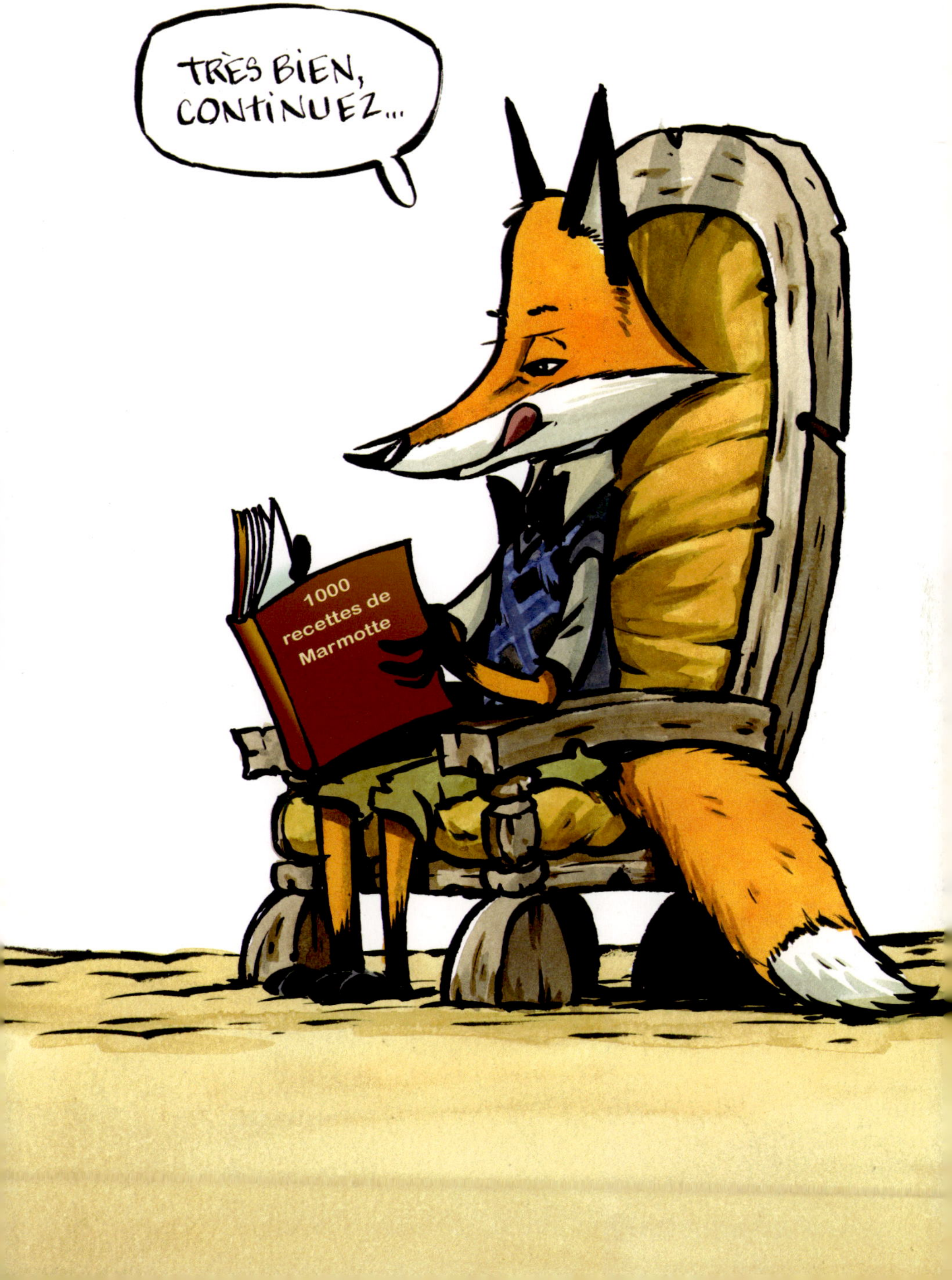
TRÈS BIEN, CONTINUEZ...
1000 recettes de Marmotte

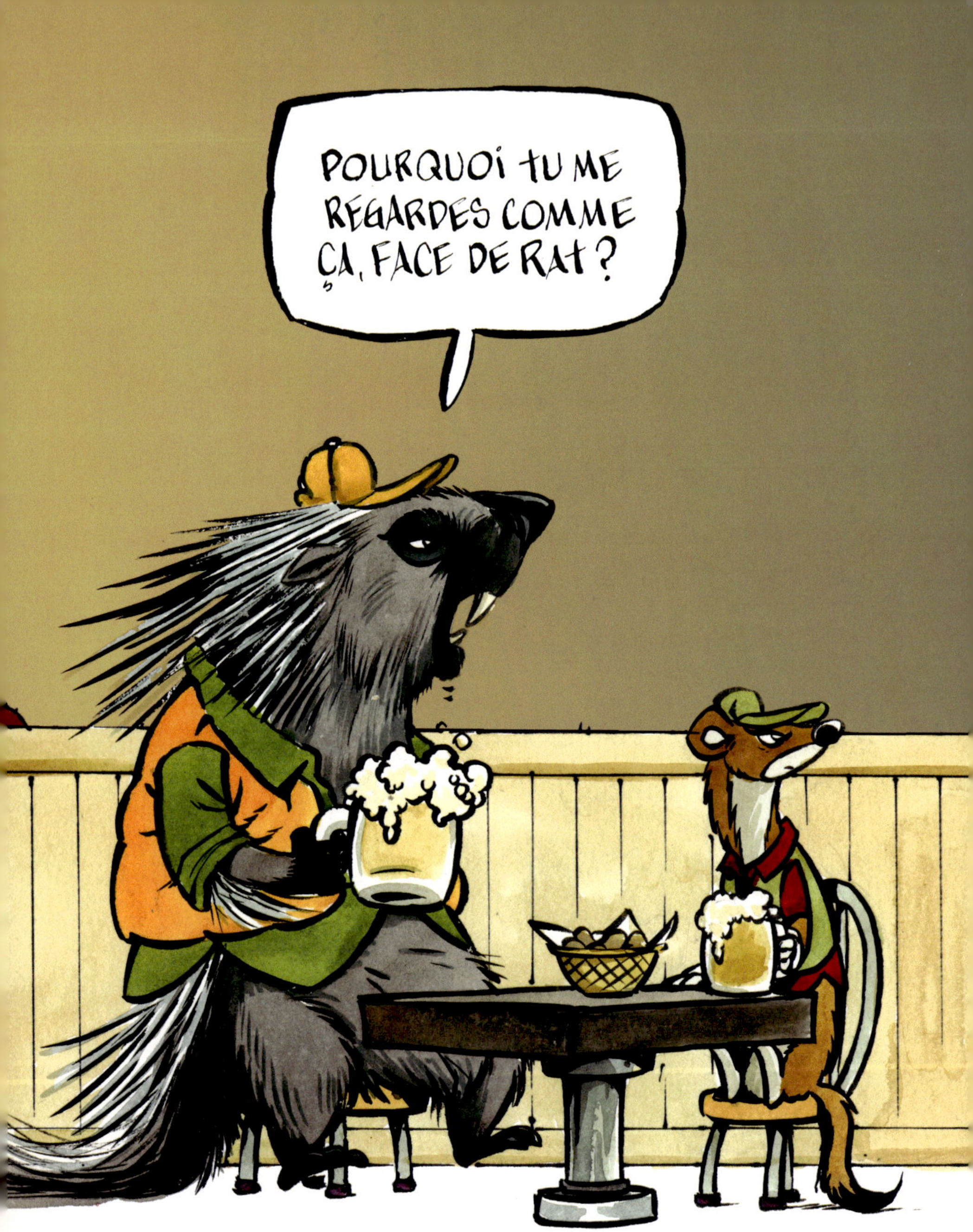
POURQUOI TU ME REGARDES COMME ÇA, FACE DE RAT ?

Savais-tu que la marmotte a une vue excellente ? De plus, son champ de vision est d'environ 300 degrés.

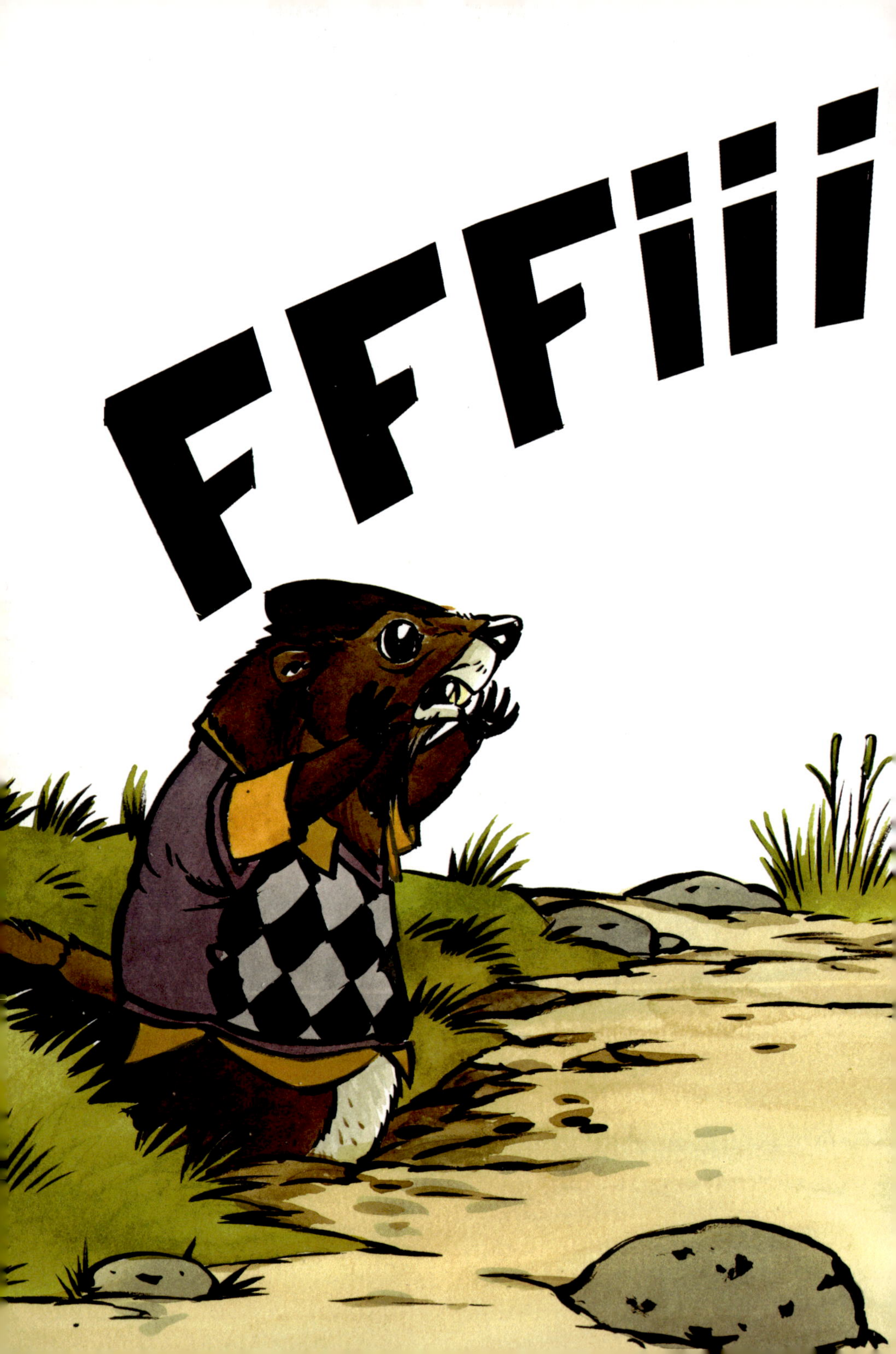
FFFiii

Savais-tu qu'en cas de danger, la marmotte émet un sifflement strident ? C'est d'ailleurs ce signal d'alarme caractéristique qui lui a valu, en certains endroits, son nom commun de «siffleux».

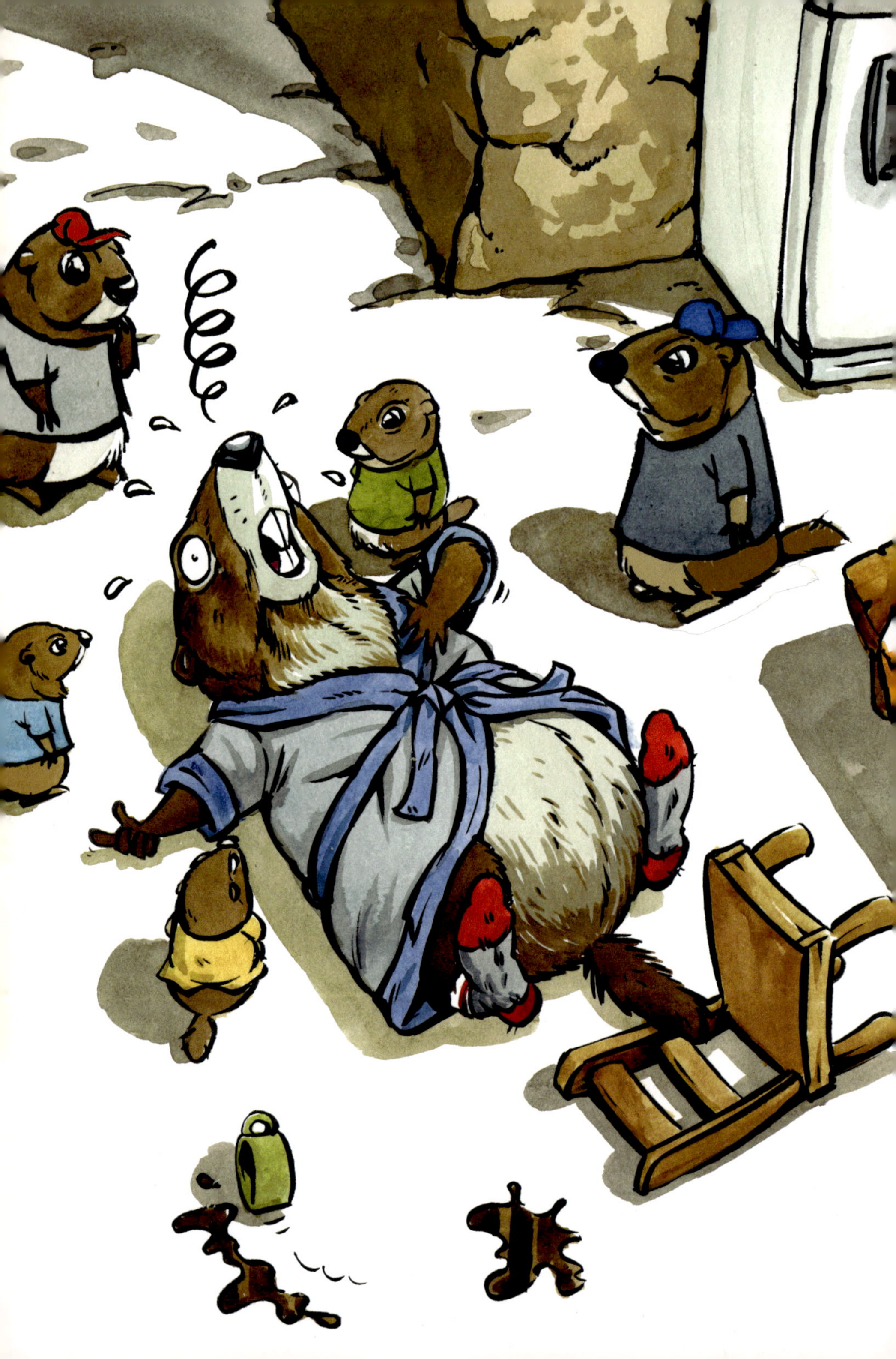

Savais-tu que les marmottes vivent en colonies d'une dizaine d'individus ? Ces groupes sont généralement constitués de quelques adultes, des petits de l'année et des jeunes de l'année précédente.

Savais-tu que, de toutes les espèces, seule la marmotte commune préfère la solitude à la vie de groupe ? Elle vit en Amérique du Nord.

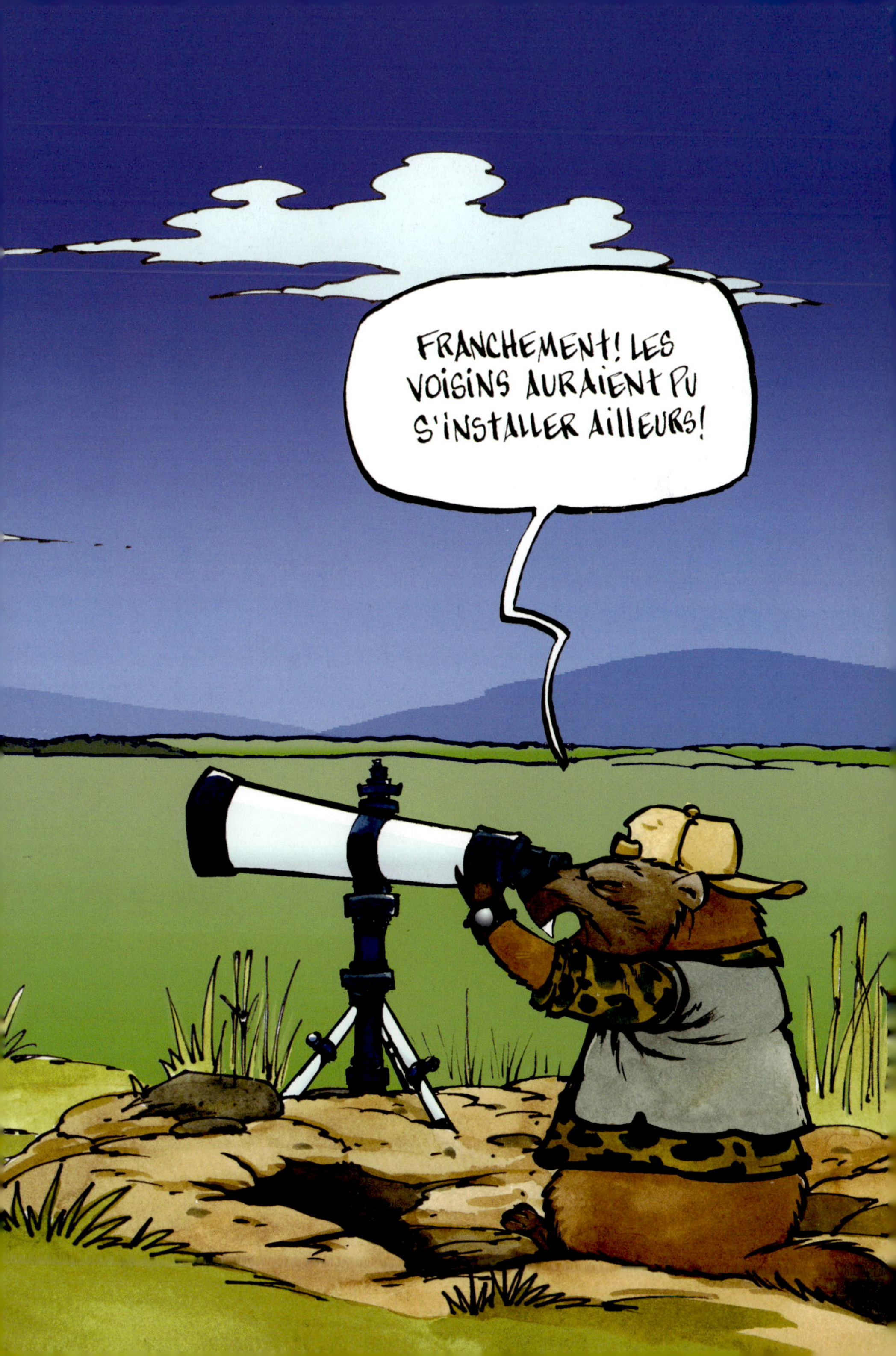
FRANCHEMENT! LES VOISINS AURAIENT PU S'INSTALLER AILLEURS!

Savais-tu que, durant l'été, les marmottes accumulent des réserves de graisse ? Ainsi, en l'espace de six mois, elles doubleront de poids.

OUI! C'EST CELLE QUE VOUS AVEZ MISE DE CÔTÉ LE PRINTEMPS DERNIER...
SOLDE 50%

Savais-tu que, l'hiver, pour survivre au froid et pallier le manque de nourriture, les marmottes hibernent ?

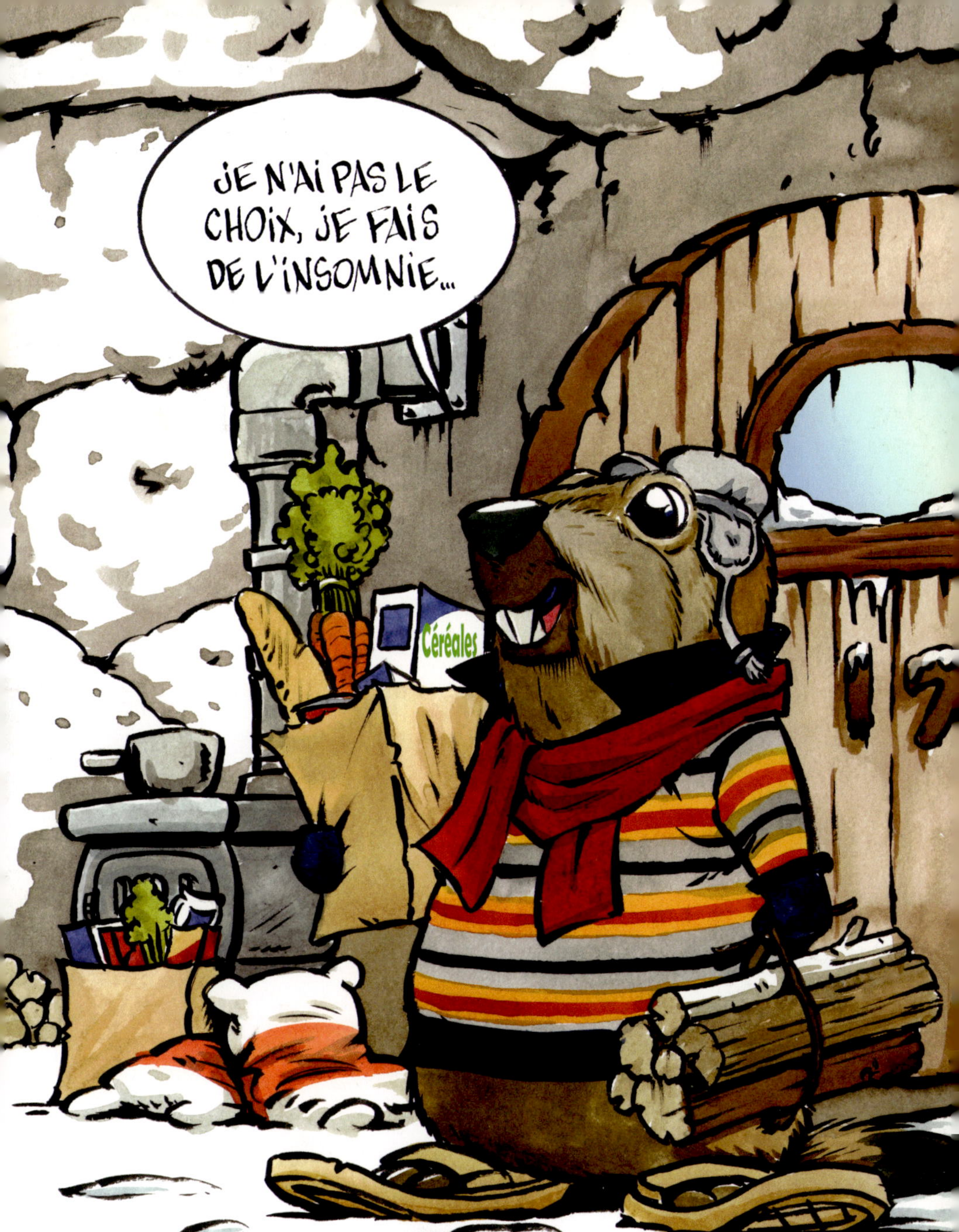
JE N'AI PAS LE CHOIX, JE FAIS DE L'INSOMNIE...
Céréales

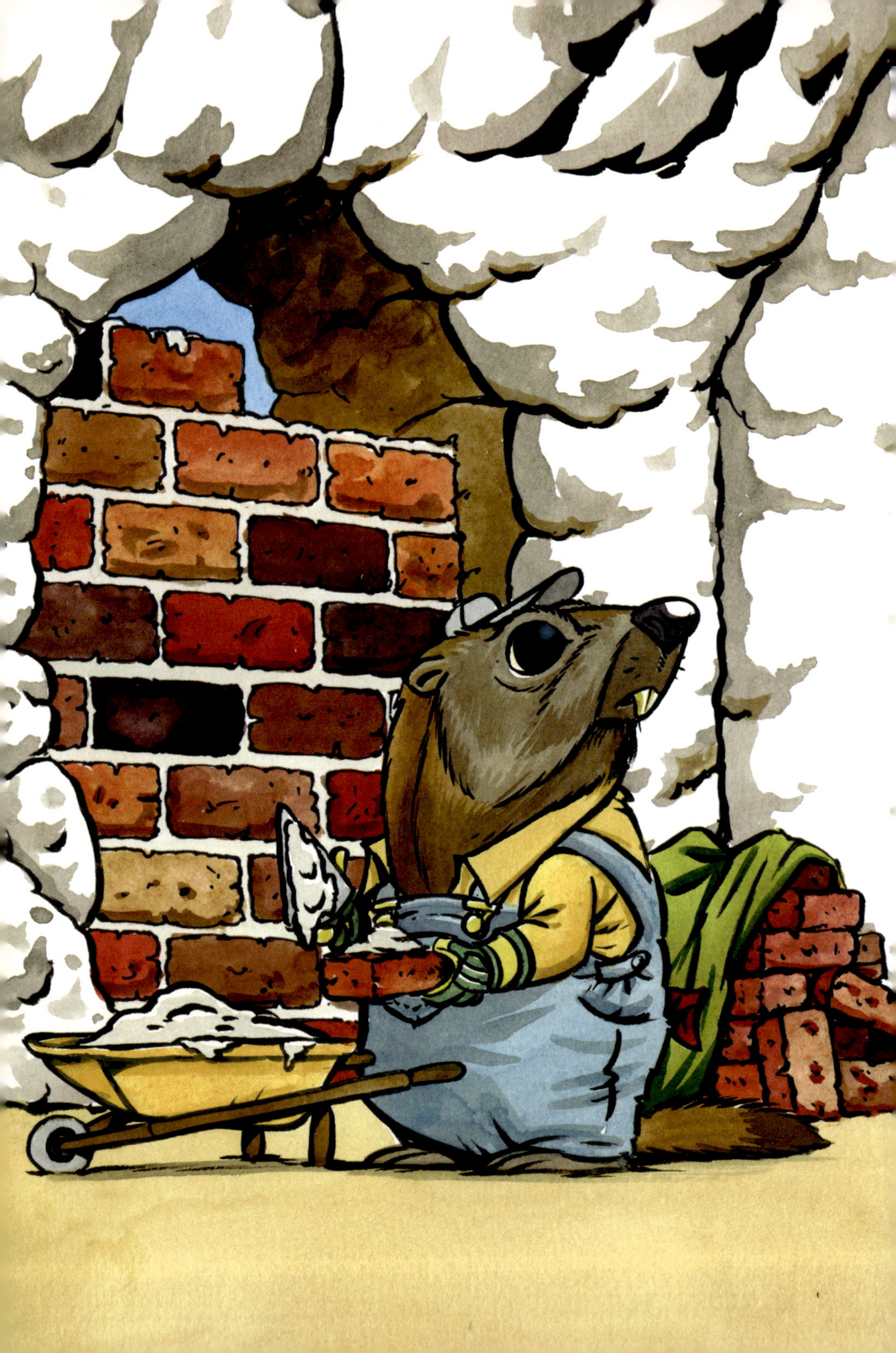

Savais-tu que, quand l'hiver arrive, la marmotte colmate les entrées de son terrier de l'intérieur avec de la terre et des herbes ? L'isolation du terrier sera assurée par le manteau de neige au sol.

Savais-tu que la marmotte s'endort roulée en boule ? Dans cette position, ses pertes de chaleur sont quasi nulles, car la sphère est la forme géométrique qui offre la plus petite surface de contact avec l'extérieur.

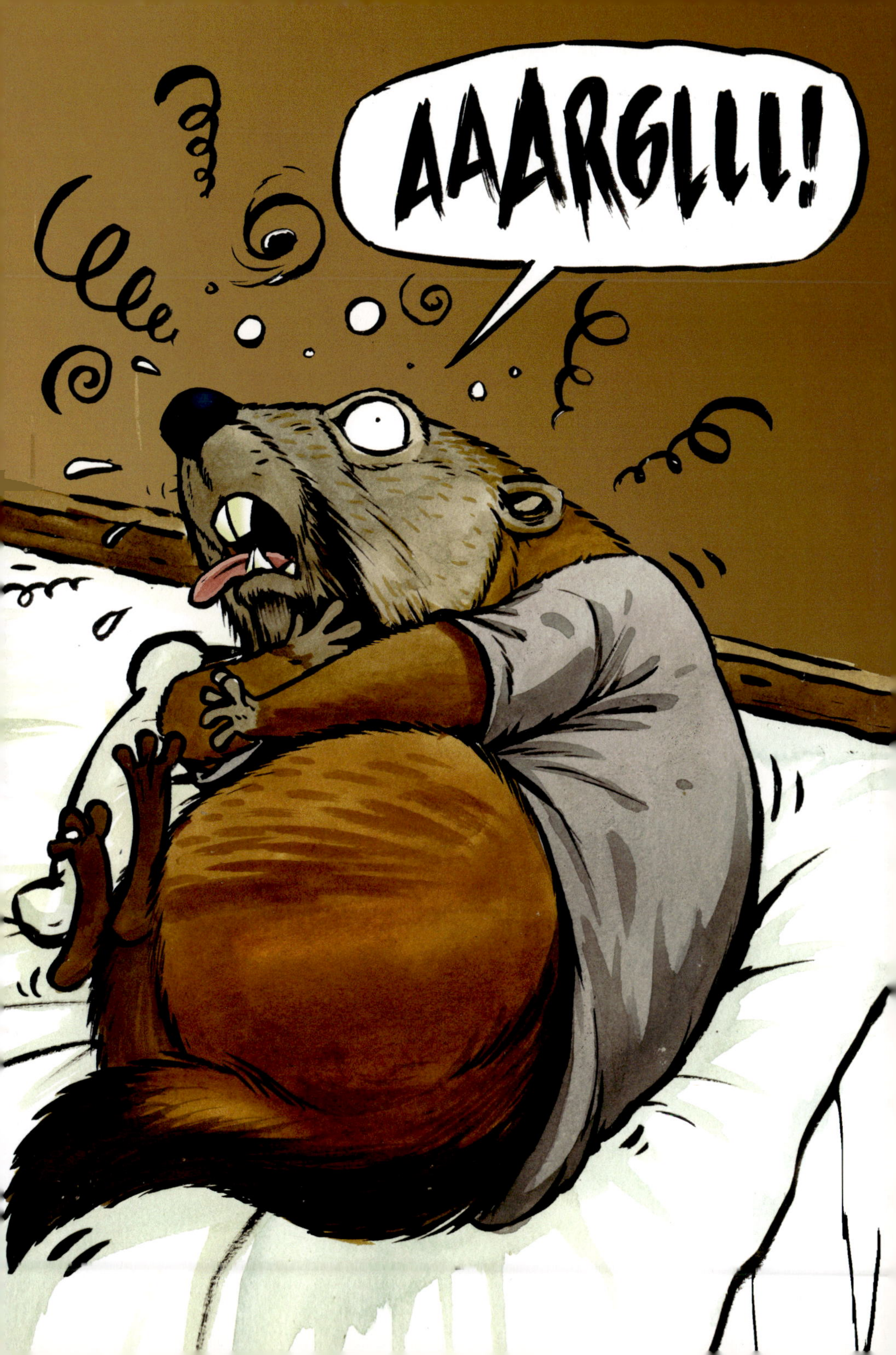
AAARGLLL!

Savais-tu que les marmottes sont de vraies hibernantes ? Pour dépenser le moins d'énergie possible, elles ralentissent leur métabolisme. Leur température corporelle chute de 37,5 °C à 5 °C.

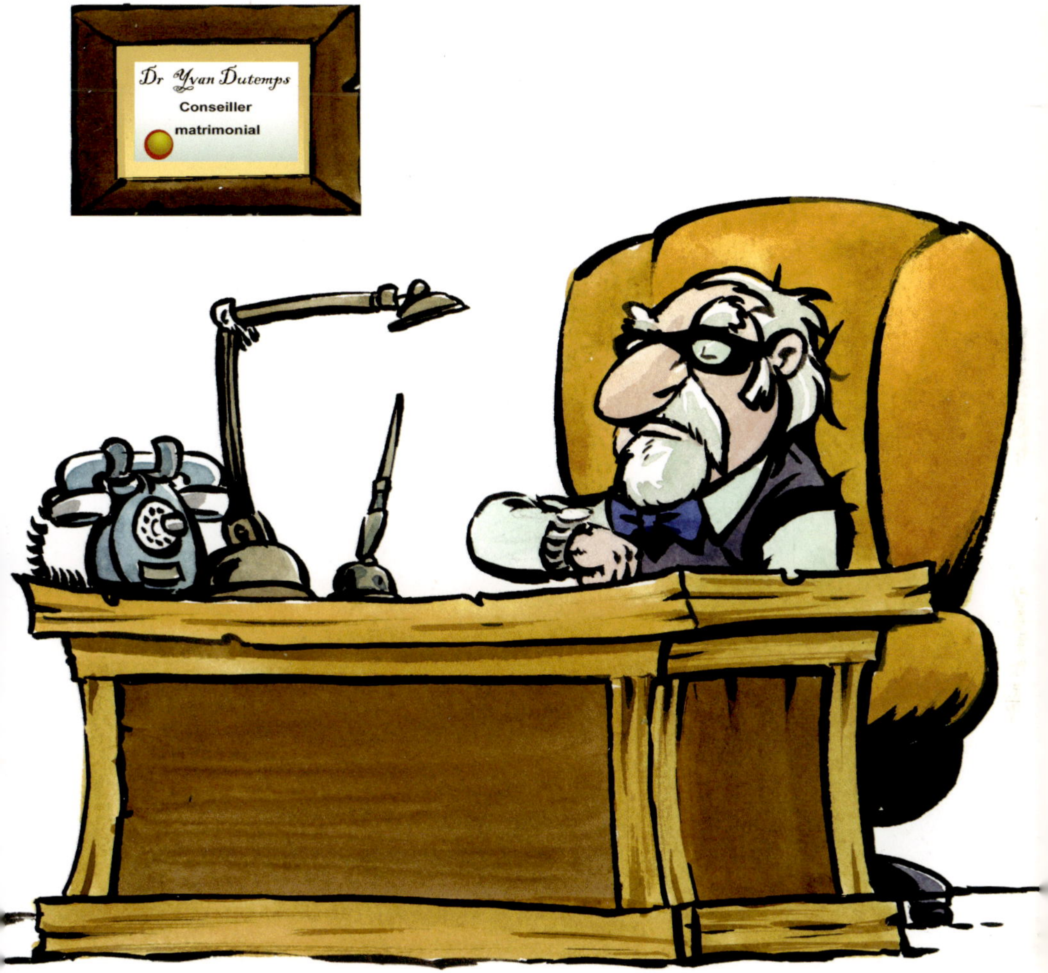
Dr Yvan Dutemps
Conseiller
matrimonial

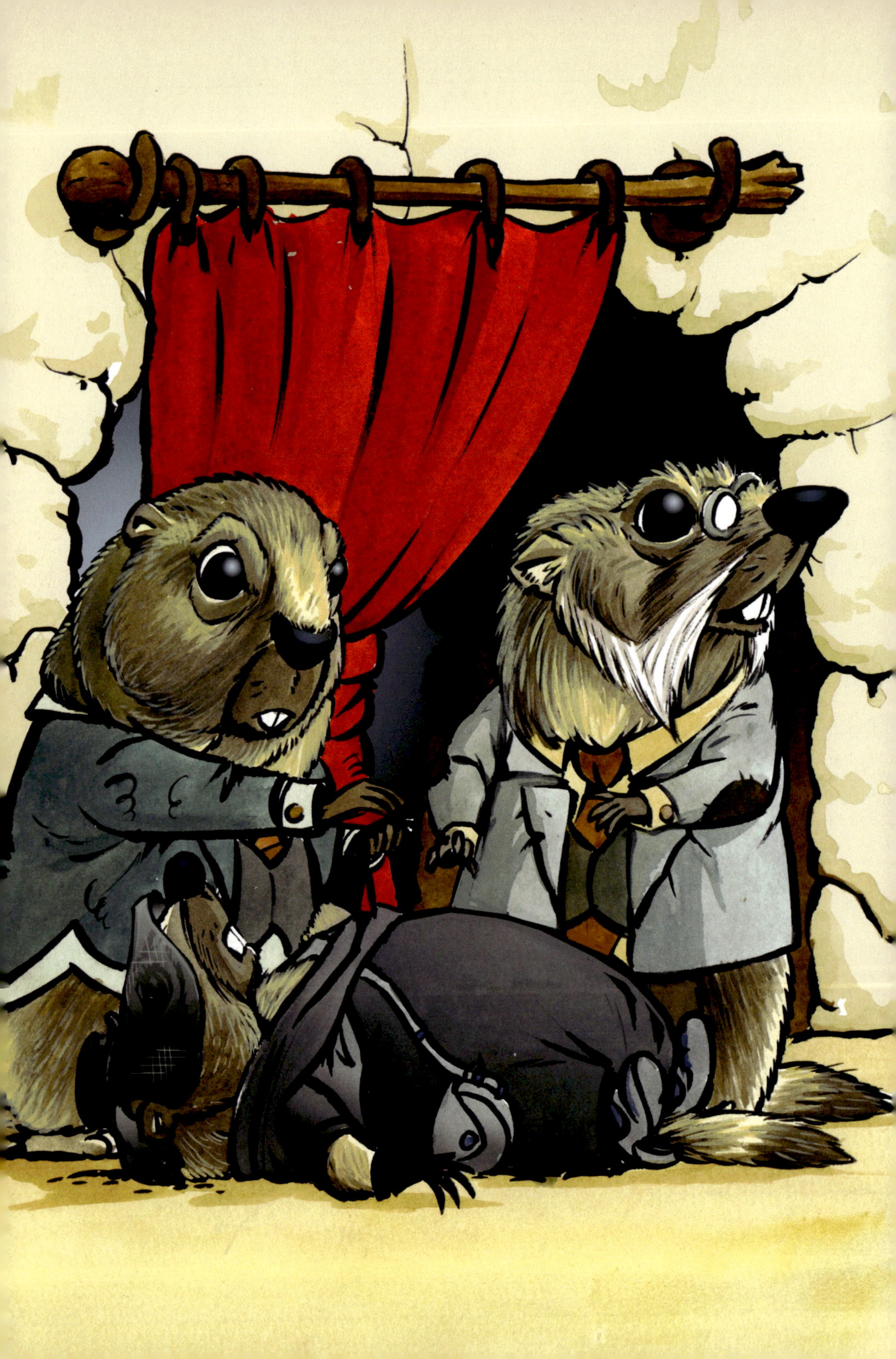

Savais-tu que, durant ce long sommeil hivernal, leurs battements cardiaques passent de 140 à 4 par minute et leur respiration de 16 inspirations à 1 à la minute ?

Savais-tu que la marmotte ne dort pas tout l'hiver ? Elle se réveille environ toutes les trois semaines pour, entre autres, déféquer et uriner. Ces courts moments exigent d'elle des efforts qui correspondent à 90 % de l'énergie qu'elle dépensera pendant l'hiver.

OUAAAAH! J'AI DORMI COMME UN BÉBÉ!
JE N'AI MÊME PAS EU BESOIN DE ME LEVER UNE SEULE FOIS CET HIVER...

Savais-tu que, quand la température du terrier descend près de 0 °C, la marmotte se réveille et augmente son métabolisme ? Elle dépense alors ses réserves de graisse en plus grande quantité.

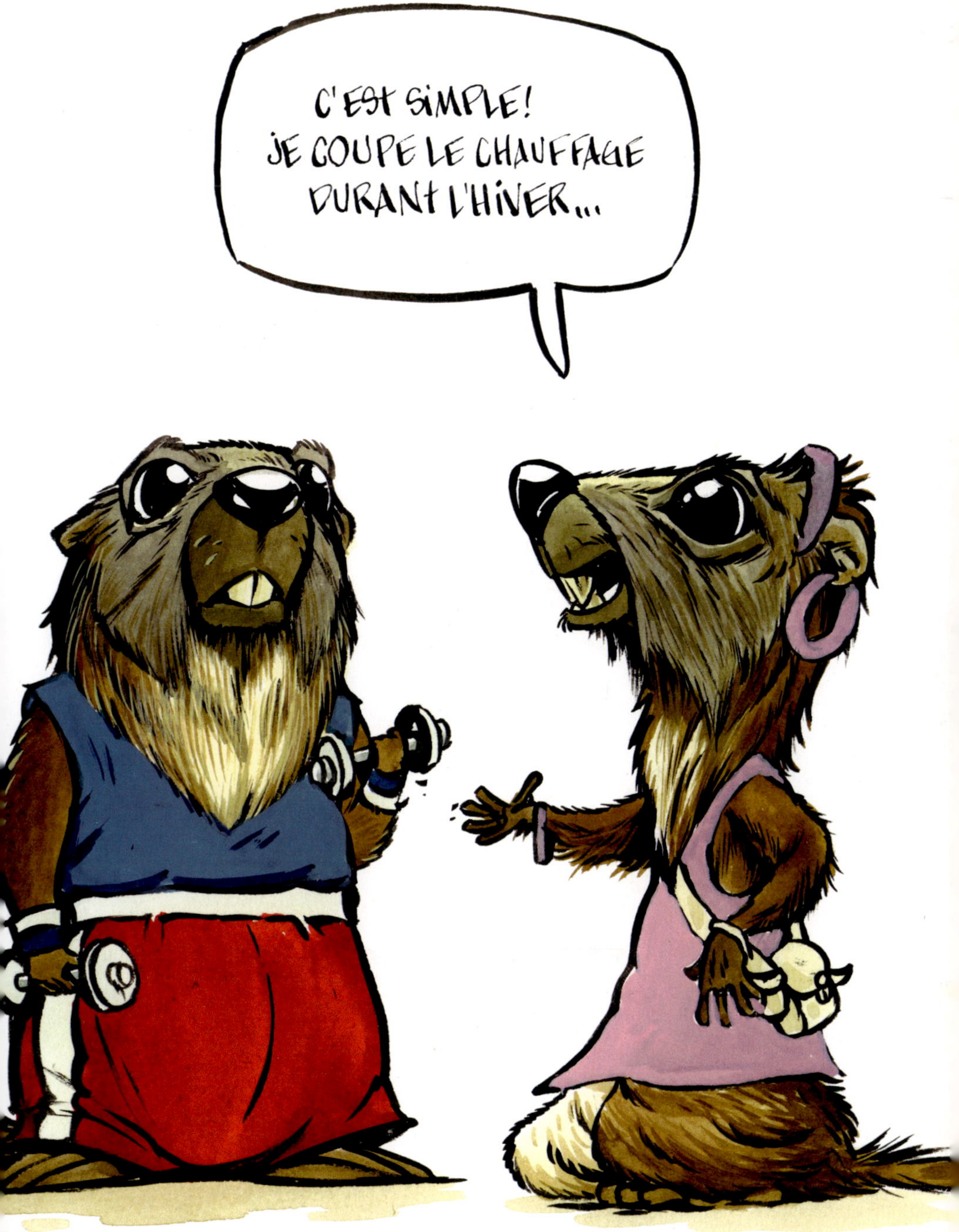
C'EST SIMPLE! JE COUPE LE CHAUFFAGE DURANT L'HIVER...

MAIS JE VOULAIS SEULEMENT DÉBLAYER L'ENTRÉE DE MON VOISIN!
PAS DU TOUT! C'EST UNE TENTATIVE DE MEURTRE!

Savais-tu que cela peut lui être fatal, certaines années où il y a de grands froids sur de longues périodes et peu de neige pour bien isoler son terrier ?

Savais-tu qu'en Amérique du Nord, chaque année, le 2 février on célèbre le « jour de la Marmotte » ? Selon la tradition, ce jour-là, la marmotte commune sort de son terrier et, si elle voit son ombre, cela annonce un printemps tardif.

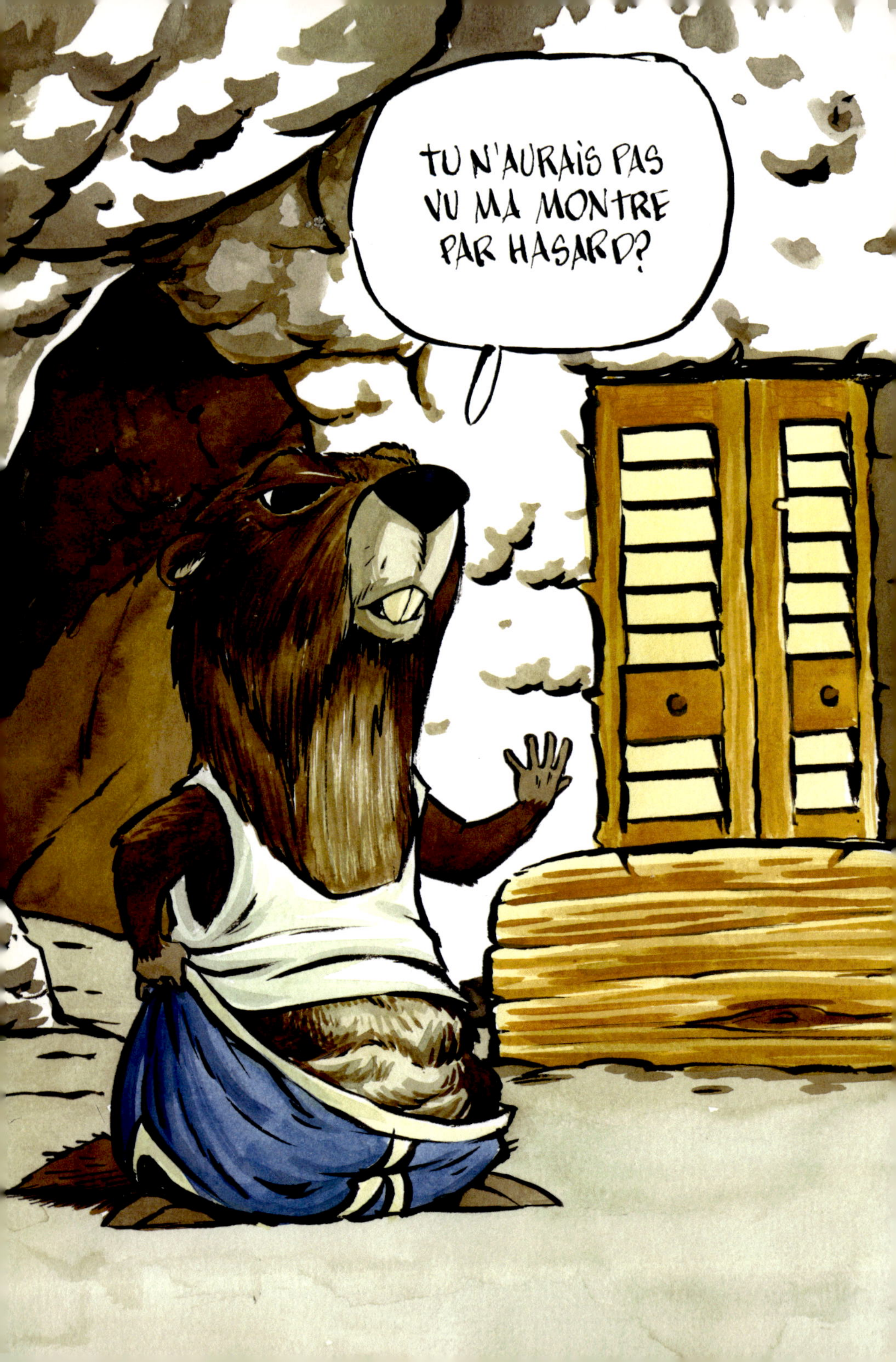
TU N'AURAIS PAS VU MA MONTRE PAR HASARD?

Savais-tu qu'au printemps, lorsque les marmottes émergent de leur profond sommeil, elles ont perdu jusqu'à la moitié de leur poids?

Savais-tu que tous les changements physiologiques qui s'opèrent chez la marmotte au cours de l'hibernation font d'elle l'objet de nombreuses recherches d'ordre médical ?

TU N'AS PAS HONTE DE PRENDRE LA PLACE DES AUTRES? TU N'ES PAS UN RAT DE LABORATOIRE!
ET T'AS VRAIMENT MAUVAISE HALEINE!

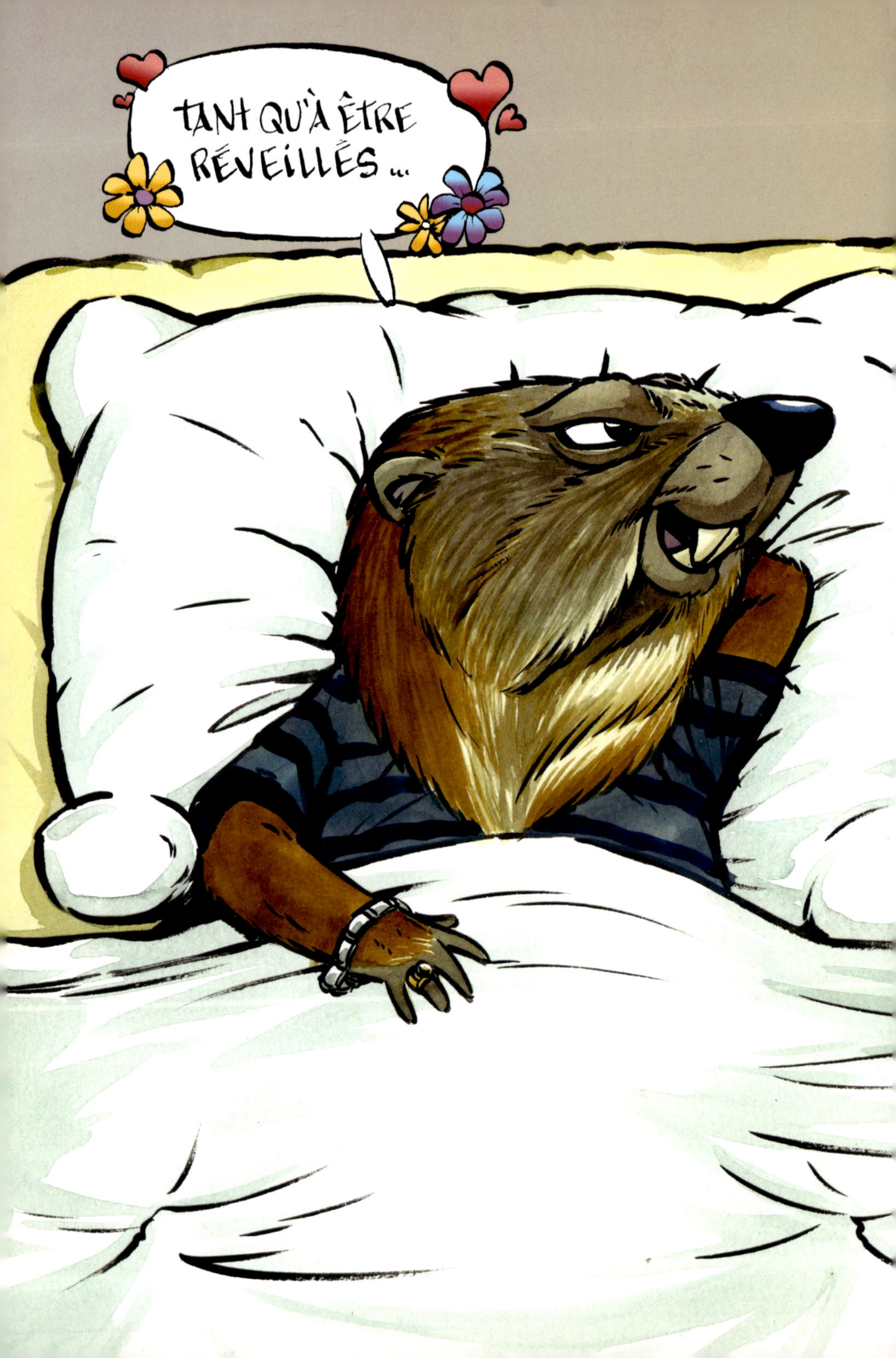
TANT QU'À ÊTRE RÉVEILLÉS ...

Savais-tu que c'est au printemps, dès leur réveil et à l'intérieur même du terrier, que les marmottes s'accouplent généralement ?

Savais-tu que, après la gestation qui dure un mois, la femelle donne naissance à quatre petits marmottons ? Certaines portées peuvent compter jusqu'à huit petits.

JE COMPRENDS, MAINTENANT, POURQUOI TU VEUX TANT CHANGER LES COUCHES... ESPÈCE DE GOURMAND!

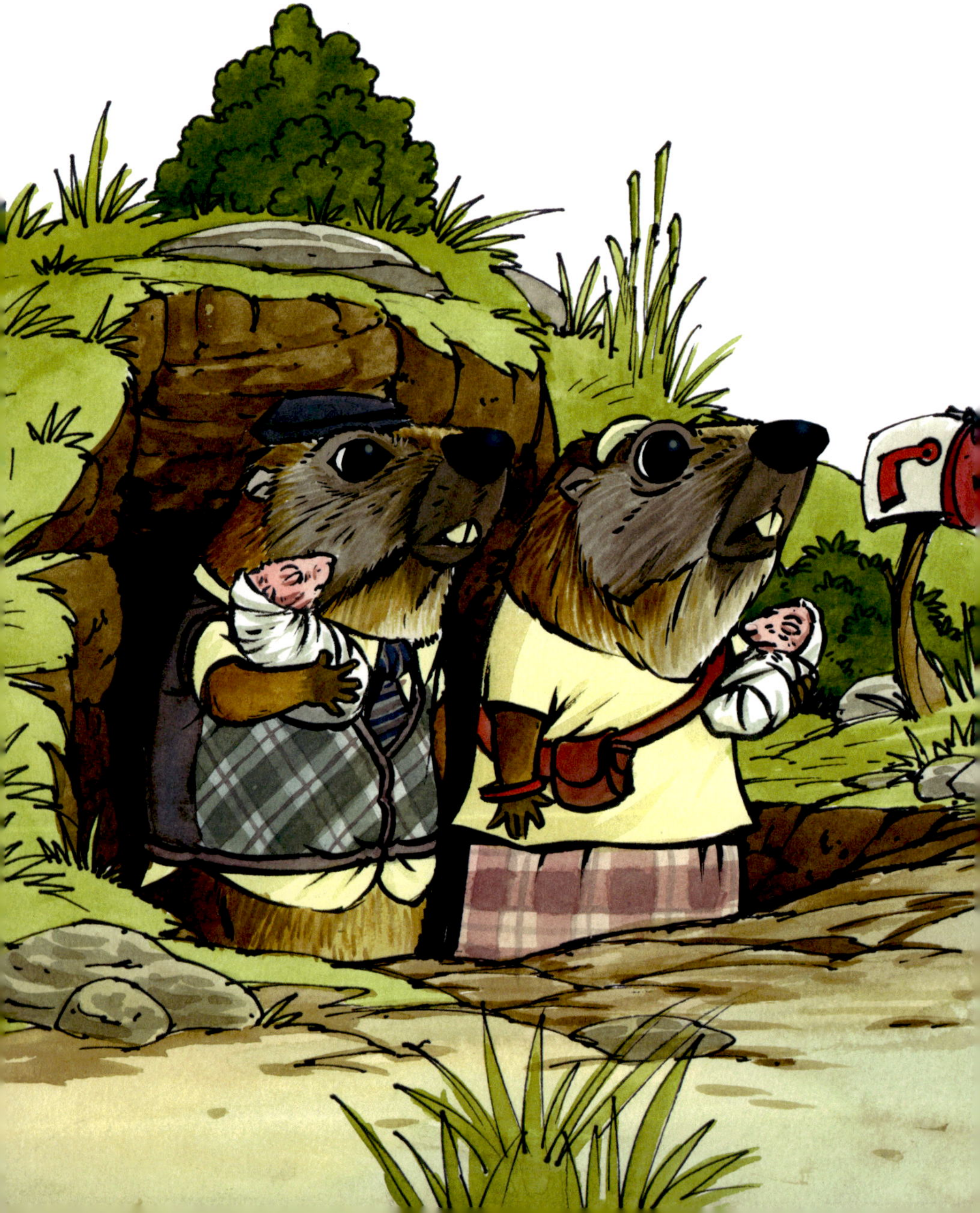

Savais-tu que les marmottes naissent nues, aveugles, sourdes, sans dents et sans défense? Dès l'âge de six semaines, elles sont couvertes de fourrure et suffisamment indépendantes pour s'aventurer hors du gîte.

Savais-tu que l'homme chasse les marmottes pour leur viande, leur fourrure et pour limiter les dégâts qu'elles font aux cultures? Elles doivent aussi se méfier, entre autres, du coyote, du renard et de l'aigle.

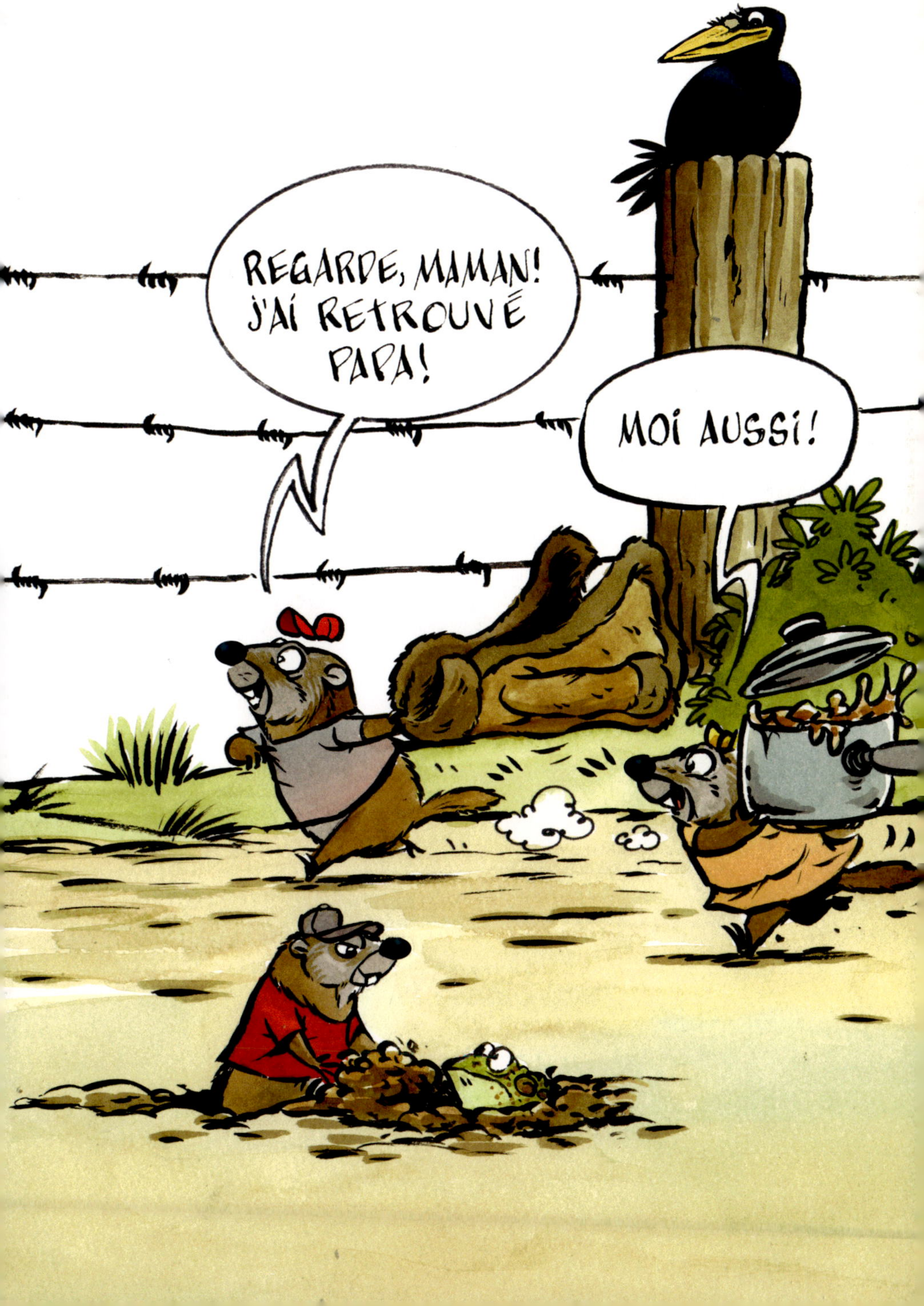
REGARDE, MAMAN! J'AI RETROUVÉ PAPA!
MOI AUSSI!

SAVAIS-TU qu'il y a d'autres titres ?

Les Dinosaures	Les Rats	Les Piranhas	Les Crocodiles
Les Sangsues	Les Crapauds	Les Serpents	Les Hyènes
Les Corneilles	Les Scorpions	Les Caméléons	Les Diables de Tasmanie
Les Goélands	Les Pieuvres	Les Dragons de Komodo	Les Mantes religieuses
Les Murènes	Les Renards	Les Chauves-souris	

TOUT EN COULEURS

What can we observe about matter?

Look around you. Everything you see is made of matter. What is matter? Matter is anything that has mass and takes up space. We can observe that matter has physical qualities, or properties. Some of these physical properties are hardness, color, taste, size, shape, odor, and texture. Our senses of sight, hearing, taste, smell, and touch help us observe the physical properties of matter.

Let's observe an apple. You can see that it has a red color and a round shape. It's about the same size as your palm. The apple is hard. But it's not too hard to bite! You taste the sweetness. You smell the fresh odor of the fruit. These are some of the physical properties of the apple.

This is an apple. It is made of matter.

What is temperature?

Temperature is another physical property of matter. <mark>Temperature</mark> is a measure of how hot or cold something is. We measure temperature with a thermometer.

There are two scales, or systems, that measure temperature. On the Celsius scale, water freezes at 0 °C. It boils at 100 °C. On the Fahrenheit scale, water freezes at 32 °F and boils at 212 °F.

When something has a low temperature, it feels cold. On a snowy day in January, the air temperature might be −6.6 °C (20 °F). When something has a high temperature, it feels hot. The air temperature in August might be 43.3 °C (110 °F).

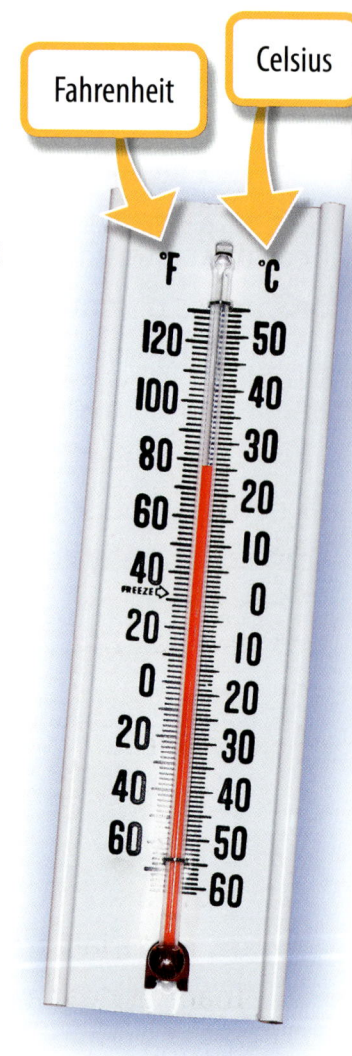

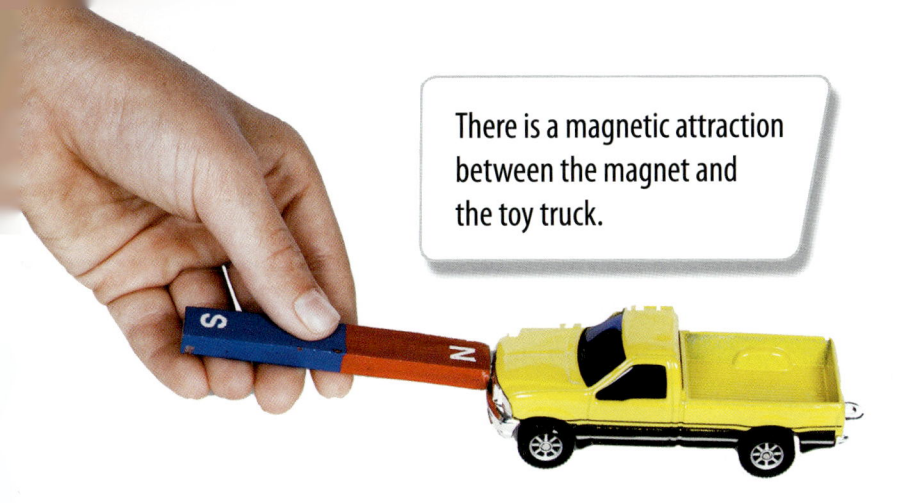

There is a magnetic attraction between the magnet and the toy truck.

What is magnetism?

Magnetism is another physical property of matter. Magnetism is a property that allows a material to become a magnet or to be attracted by a magnet. Something that is magnetic pulls, or attracts, other objects toward itself. Long ago, people observed a rock called lodestone. They found out that lodestone was magnetic. People made magnets out of lodestones.

Iron, steel, and nickel are metals. They are all attracted by magnets. If you put them near a magnet, they will move toward the magnet.

Most materials are not magnetic. Wood is not magnetic. Put a magnet near a piece of wood. The wood does not move toward the magnet. Paper, plastic, and glass are also not magnetic.

How can we measure matter?

<mark>Mass</mark> is the amount of matter an object has. You can use a pan balance to measure an object's mass. Put the object you want to measure on one side. Add the masses you know to the other side. Add masses until the two sides balance. Add the numbers of the known masses. Now you know the mass of the object.

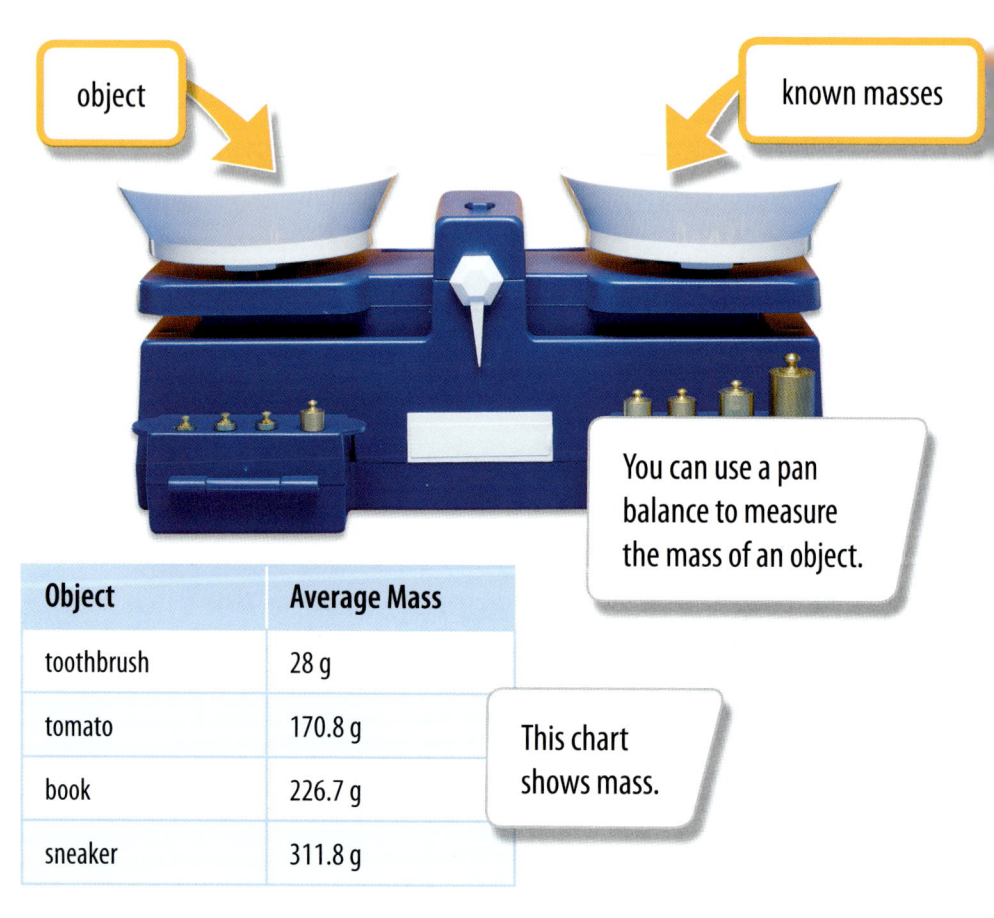

object

known masses

You can use a pan balance to measure the mass of an object.

Object	Average Mass
toothbrush	28 g
tomato	170.8 g
book	226.7 g
sneaker	311.8 g

This chart shows mass.

6

volume with egg

volume without egg

You can use a beaker of water to measure an object's volume. Volume is the amount of space that an object takes up. Let's measure the volume of an egg. Put 300 ml of water in a beaker. Now put the egg in the beaker. The water level goes up to 350 ml. The egg has increased the level of the water. Subtract the two numbers. You find that the volume of the egg is 50 ml.

You can use a metric ruler to measure the volume of a solid in the shape of a rectangle. The width of a book is 15 cm. Its length is 23 cm. Its height is 5 cm. Multiply the numbers. $15 \times 23 \times 5 = 1,725$. The volume of the book is 1,725 cubic centimeters.

7

Why do some objects float?

Some objects float because of their density. Density is the amount of matter an object has compared to the space it takes up.

Put a piece of wood in a beaker of water. Notice that the wood floats. Its density is less than the density of water. Now take the wood out of the water. Cut it into pieces. Have an adult supervise you. Put one piece of the wood back in the water. What happens? The piece floats. Why? A small piece of an object has the same density as the whole object.

These objects are all less dense than water. Each object will float.
- plastic bottle cap
- piece of wax
- cork
- wooden block
- piece of dental floss
- plastic bag

These objects will all float in water. Can you think of some other objects that will float?

Objects that are more dense than water will sink.

Why do some objects sink?

Some objects sink because of their density. Every object is made up of tiny particles of matter. When these particles are close together, the object has more density. Objects that are more dense than water will sink in water.

Put a marble in a beaker of water. The marble will sink. Its density is more than the density of water. Sometimes two similar objects can have different densities. A table tennis ball and a golf ball are both balls. A table tennis ball will float. But a golf ball has a greater density than water. It will sink.

These objects are all more dense than water. They will all sink.
- penny or other coin
- marble
- golf ball
- bar of soap
- paper clip
- peanut

9

How can we classify water?

We can classify water by its three states, or forms. The three states are solid, liquid, and gas.

A **solid** is matter with a definite volume and shape. When water is in a solid state it has a definite volume. Solid water also has a definite shape. An ice cube is solid water. It is often in the shape of a rectangle or a square. A snowball is solid water. It is round.

Have you ever gone ice-skating, or seen ice skaters? The ice on the skating rink is a solid. It takes the shape of the rink. A huge glacier is a solid. It is a large body of frozen water. A tiny snowflake also is solid water.

A snowflake is one of the solid states of water.

10

A <mark>liquid</mark> has a definite volume, but its shape is not definite. When water is in a liquid state, it has a definite volume. But it does not have a definite shape. If water is in a container, like a glass, it will take the shape of that container. A swimming pool is full of liquid water. The water takes the shape of the pool. Rain is liquid water. It is in the form of tiny drops.

A <mark>gas</mark> does not have a definite volume. It also doesn't have a definite shape. You can't see gas. A gas simply fills up all the space it is in, no matter how big the container is. Water has a gas form. It is called water vapor.

Water can change from one state to another. It can change from a liquid to a solid. It can change from a solid to a liquid. Water can also change from a liquid to a gas.

water vapor

liquid water

solid water

liquid water

How does heating change water?

The temperature of water can increase when there is more heat energy. There is a physical change when water is heated. Solid water is changed to a liquid state when heated. Suppose you have an ice cube. You put it in a dish on the kitchen table. The ice cube starts to warm up. The particles in the ice cube move apart. The ice cube melts. Now you have a dish of liquid water.

Large bodies of solid water can also melt. Picture a warm day in March. You want to ice skate on the lake. The lake was frozen last week. This week, the weather is warmer. Heat energy from the sun warms the lake. The ice changes from a solid to a liquid state. No ice skating!

Heating changes liquid water to a gas. The process of liquid changing into a gas is called **evaporation**. Heat energy warms the water. The particles of the water move faster. Particles in the water bump into the particles on the top. The particles on the top go into the air. These particles turn into a gas.

When the water temperature goes up, the particles of water move faster and faster. Evaporation speeds up. Eventually the water boils. Bubbles of water vapor form and move to the surface. The water vapor rises into the air.

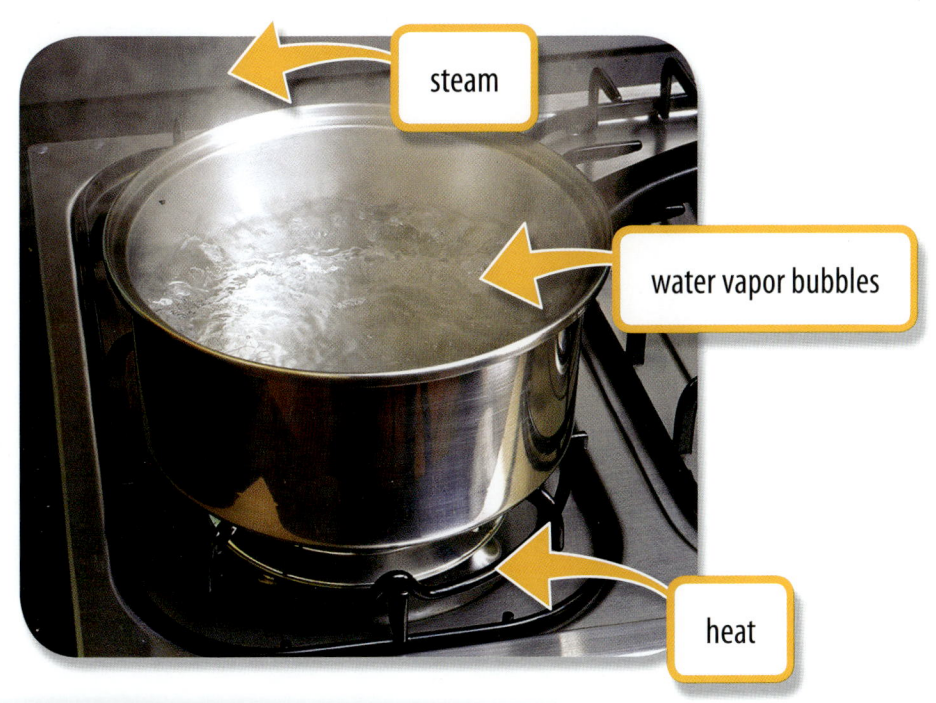

steam

water vapor bubbles

heat

How does cooling change water?

The temperature of water can decrease when there is less heat energy. Suppose you have an empty ice cube tray. You fill it with liquid water. You put the tray in the freezer. The temperature in the freezer is very low, so the water has a physical change. <u>When water gets very cold, its particles move closer together. The water freezes.</u> Now you have solid water. You have made ice cubes.

Even very large amounts of liquid water can freeze. Picture a cold day in December. You look at a pond. The pond was liquid water last week. This week, the temperature is lower. There is not as much heat energy from the sun. What happens? That's right! The liquid water starts to turn to ice. The temperature may get lower. If it does, more ice will form.

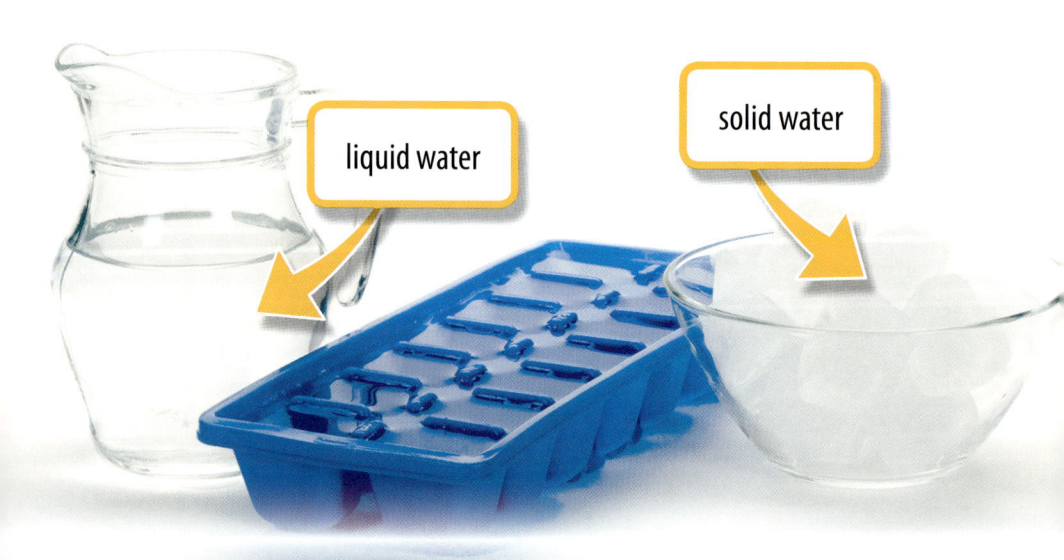

liquid water

solid water

Cooling changes water vapor to liquid water. **Condensation** is the process by which a gas changes into a liquid.

Suppose you put ice cubes in a glass. Then you put liquid water in the glass. Look at the outside of the glass. The outside of the glass is dry. Wait a few minutes. There are tiny drops of water on the glass. Why? There is water vapor in the air. Some of the water vapor condenses on the cold glass. The water vapor changes to liquid water.

Look at the clouds in the sky. How do they form? Warm air with water vapor in it rises. The temperature gets cooler. The warm air cools. The water vapor condenses. It forms drops of water. The drops come together and form clouds.

water vapor

solid water

liquid water

If you cut an apple, you cause a physical change. But the apple does not change into something else.

How can matter change?

There can be physical changes in matter. However, the matter is still the same substance.

Cutting causes a physical change. You have a whole apple. You cut it into pieces. But the pieces are still an apple.

Folding causes a physical change. You have a tissue. You fold it into a square. It's still a tissue.

You know that matter can be solid, liquid, or gas. Matter can change its state but still be the same substance. For example, melting causes a change of state. A dish of ice cream begins to warm up and melt into a liquid. The liquid is still ice cream.

Freezing causes a change of state. You put a bowl of soup in the freezer. The soup changes from a liquid to a solid, but it is still soup.

You can reuse or recycle matter. For example, you can reuse an aluminum can. Clean it out and decorate the outside. Then put pencils in it. Now it's a pencil holder. You can also reuse a plastic bottle. Cut off the top. Put dirt in the bottom. Add some flower seeds. Now you have a flower pot.

We recycle a lot of paper. The old paper is shredded and mixed into a pulp. The pulp becomes new newspapers, paper plates, or toilet paper.

Glass can be recycled over and over. Melted glass is used for new jars or glasses. Crushed glass may be used in bricks. It may become part of a new road.

Recycled plastic has many uses. Your old bottles may turn into a swing set! Recycled plastic may be used to make toys and other objects.

How can newspaper be reused or recycled?

How many different substances can you see in this mixture?

What is a mixture?

A <mark>mixture</mark> is a combination of two or more different substances that retain their identities. This means that the substances stay the same. No new substance is made. Making a mixture is a physical change. Solids, liquids, and gases can all form mixtures.

You add fruit to your cereal. Now you have a mixture of two solids. You add milk. Now you have a mixture of solids and a liquid.

Look around. You can see all kinds of mixtures. Many rocks are a mixture of minerals. You can often see each of the minerals in the rock.

How do you make a mixture? Put some sand in a pail. Add some rocks. Stir or shake the pail. Now you have a mixture. Pick up a handful of the mixture. The sand will fall through your fingers. The rocks will stay in your hand. The rocks and sand each retain their own identity. They remain what they are.

Make another mixture. Put some sand in a jar. Add water. Put on the lid. Shake it up. At first, the water and sand look like they are mixed together. But let the jar sit still for a few minutes. The sand will sink to the bottom. The water and sand keep their own identities.

water

sand

Sand and water form a mixture. Each substance keeps its own identity.

What is a solution?

A <mark>solution</mark> <u>is a mixture that has the same composition throughout because all the parts are mixed evenly.</u> The larger part of a solution dissolves the other parts. It is called a solvent. Water is a solvent. A solute is a smaller part of a solution. A solute dissolves in the solvent. For example, sugar is a solute that dissolves in water, a solvent.

A solution can be a mixture of a solid and a liquid. The solution will be a liquid.

A solution can also be a liquid and a liquid. Rubbing alcohol is a solution. It is a mixture of water and another liquid called isopropanol.

A solution can also be a gas and a liquid. Carbon dioxide is a gas. Mix it with water. You get soda water.

You can add liquid food coloring to water to make a solution.

Water is a solvent. Food coloring is a solute. When food coloring is added to water, the result is a solution.

    A solution can be made with two solids. The solids are melted, and then mixed together. A penny is made from copper and zinc. A dime is made from copper and nickel.

    Here's how to make a solution. Put some sugar in a jar. The sugar is the solute. Add water. The water is the solvent. Shake the jar. You see the solid and liquid begin to mix. Put the jar on the table. You can't tell the water from the sugar. They have mixed evenly. You know you have a solution.

Responding

Observe Sinking and Floating

Investigate sinking and floating. Work with a friend or parent. Get some objects from home or school. Get as many different materials as you can find. Use objects of different sizes and shapes.

Put water in a sink or bowl. Make a three-column chart. Write the name of each object on the chart. Will the object sink or float? Write your prediction, or what you think will happen, next to each name. Put each object in the water. Observe what happens. Was your prediction right? Write down what happened. Work with your partner. Write a paragraph to tell what happened.

Draw Pictures

Use the Internet or library. Work with a partner if you like. Find out more about how water changes states. Draw a picture of water in each state. Draw pictures to show how water changes states. Add labels to your pictures. Write a paragraph explaining how water changes states.

Glossary

condensation [kahn•duhn•SAY•shuhn] The process by which a gas changes into a liquid. *Sometimes you can see condensation on a window.*

density [DEN•suh•tee] The amount of matter in an object compared to the space it takes up. *A plastic bottle cap floats because its density is less than the density of water.*

evaporation [ee•vap•uh•RAY•shuhn] The process by which a liquid changes into a gas. *Steam coming from a tea kettle is an example of evaporation.*

gas [GAS] The state of matter that does not have a definite shape or volume. *Most of the time you can't see a gas.*

liquid [LIK•wid] The state of matter that has a definite volume but no definite shape. *Liquid water takes the shape of a glass.*

magnetism [MAG•ni•tiz•uhm] The physical property of being magnetic. *There is no magnetism between wood and a magnet.*

mass [MASS] The amount of matter an object has. *The grapefruit has a larger mass than the orange.*

matter [MAT·er] Anything that has mass and takes up space. *Everything around us is made of matter.*

mixture [MIKS·cher] A combination of two or more different substances that retain their identities. *The fruit salad is a mixture of grapes, apples, and cherries.*

solid [SAHL·id] The state of matter that has a definite shape and a definite volume. *My desk is a solid made of wood.*

solution [suh·LOO·shun] A mixture that has the same composition throughout because all the parts are mixed evenly. *Sweet ice tea is a solution made of tea, lemon juice, and sugar.*

temperature [TEM·pur·uh·chur] A measure of how hot or cold something is. *Ice cream is kept at a cold temperature.*

volume [VAHL·yoom] The amount of space that an object takes up. *You can measure an object to find its volume.*